DOORS AND WINDOWS

THE ENCHANTED WORLD
LIBRARY OF NATIONS
HOME REPAIR AND IMPROVEMENT
CLASSICS OF EXPLORATION
PLANET EARTH
PEOPLES OF THE WILD
THE EPIC OF FLIGHT
THE SEAFARERS
WORLD WAR II
THE GOOD COOK
THE TIME-LIFE ENCYCLOPAEDIA OF GARDENING
THE GREAT CITIES
THE OLD WEST
THE WORLD'S WILD PLACES
THE EMERGENCE OF MAN
LIFE LIBRARY OF PHOTOGRAPHY
TIME-LIFE LIBRARY OF ART
GREAT AGES OF MAN
LIFE SCIENCE LIBRARY
LIFE NATURE LIBRARY
THE TIME-LIFE BOOK OF BOATING
TECHNIQUES OF PHOTOGRAPHY
LIFE AT WAR
LIFE GOES TO THE MOVIES
BEST OF LIFE
LIFE IN SPACE

This volume is part of a series offering home
owners detailed instructions on repairs,
construction and improvements which they can
undertake themselves.

HOME REPAIR
AND IMPROVEMENT

DOORS AND WINDOWS

BY THE EDITORS OF
TIME-LIFE BOOKS

TIME-LIFE BOOKS
AMSTERDAM

TIME-LIFE BOOKS
EUROPEAN EDITOR: Kit van Tulleken
Assistant European Editor: Gillian Moore
Design Director: Ed Skyner
Photography Director: Pamela Marke
Chief of Research: Vanessa Kramer
Chief Sub-Editor: Ilse Gray

HOME REPAIR AND IMPROVEMENT
EDITORIAL STAFF FOR DOORS AND WINDOWS
Editor: William Frankel
Assistant Editor: David Thiemann
Designer: Anne Masters
Picture Editor: Adrian Allen
Associate Designer: Kenneth E. Hancock
Text Editors: Richard Flanagan, John Manners, Bob Menaker
Staff Writers: Lynn Addison, Megan Barnett, Thierry Bright-Sagnier, Stephen Brown, Alan Epstein, Steven J. Forbis, Leslie Marshall, Brooke Stoddard, William Worsley
Art Associates: George Bell, Lorraine Rivard, Richard Whiting
Editorial Assistant: Susanne S. Trice

EUROPEAN EDITION
Series Director: Jackie Matthews
Writer-Researchers: Charles Boyle, Margaret Hall
Designer: William Saunders
Sub-Editors: Frances Dixon, Wendy Gibbons, Hilary Hockman

EDITORIAL PRODUCTION
Chief: Jane Hawker
Production Assistants: Nikki Allen, Maureen Kelly
Editorial Department: Theresa John, Debra Lelliott

THE CONSULTANTS: Ron Pratt, formerly a self-employed carpenter and joiner and the director of a manufacturing company supplying pre-cast concrete products to the building industry, is a lecturer in carpentry and joinery at Erith College of Technology.

Leslie Stokes was a self-employed carpenter and joiner for seven years, specializing in purpose-made joinery and internal fittings. Since 1976 he has taught in the building department at the Hammersmith and West London College.

Alan Bayliss served his apprenticeship with a leading Sydney cabinet-making firm. He worked as a carpenter and cabinet-maker for 18 years, then took a teaching diploma from Sydney College of Advanced Education. Since 1970 he has been a teacher of cabinet-making at Sydney Technical College.

Charles Hamilton, a carpenter and construction supervisor, has specialized in custom remodelling and restoration in the Washington D.C. area for more than three decades.

Contents

1   **Curing the Common Ailments**   **7**

Why Windows Stick—and How to Free Them   8

Replacing a Broken Sash Cord   14

Simple Carpentry for Everyday Door Problems   18

Working on the Architraves and Stops   23

The Glazier's Craft: Cutting and Setting Glass   34

Weatherstripping to Seal the Gaps   40

Keeping Up Appearances: Decorating Doors and Windows   44

2   **Openings for Doors and Windows**   **49**

The Anatomy of Interior and Exterior Walls   50

Framing a Doorway in a Timber-Stud Partition   52

How to Break an Opening Through a Masonry Wall   54

Cutting a Hole in the Roof   68

3   **A Wealth of Windows**   **71**

Keeping Out the Cold: Double Glazing for Existing Windows   72

A Factory-Made Unit, Complete with All Its Parts   78

Putting In a Skylight That Opens   82

The Flat-Roofed Dormer—a Window Built into the Roof   84

4   **A Door for Every Purpose**   **93**

Pre-Hung Units for Easy Fitting   94

Choosing the Right Lock   97

The Fine Art of Fitting and Hanging a Door   98

The Space Savers: Sliding Doors for Tight Places   110

A Modern Garage Door That Comes in a Kit   116

Credits and Acknowledgements   **124**

Index/Glossary   **124**

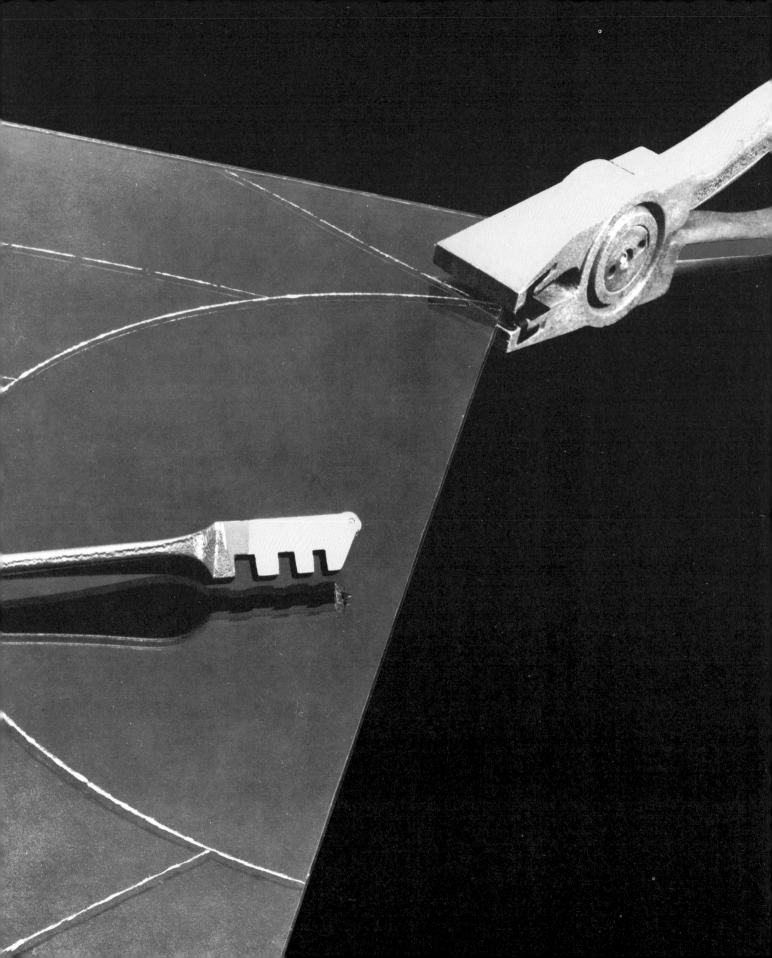

1 Curing the Common Ailments

A curved windowpane. Cutting glass to a clean curve calls for a glass cutter, a pair of special glass pliers and a steady hand. The glass is scored along a template with the carbide-tipped wheel of the cutter; then lines radiating from the curve are scored freehand, dividing the area outside the curve into several small sections. Each section is gripped in succession with the pliers—or, if pliers are not available, with one of the notches in the shaft of the cutter—and snapped along the scored lines, until the curve is completely revealed.

Windows and doors are the Achilles' heel of a house—and no wonder. These covered holes in the house walls must seal out wind, rain, snow and ice, but they must also break the seal at the touch of a hand. The walls are massive and stationary; the doors and windows, the only moving parts in the structure of the house, are intricate little machines that are designed to open and close thousands of times a year. And while walls present to the elements a single, unbroken surface, and are often rendered or sheathed with cladding for further protection, the doors and windows abound in cracks and crevices where heat, cold and moisture can enter and rot can begin. It is all a great paradox: an opening, vulnerable to all the vagaries of weather, has been deliberately set into a shelter that has been built to keep the weather out.

Every door and window is a compromise between these conflicting demands. Like most compromises it eventually breaks down—and doors and windows do in fact require frequent maintenance. The most common repairs are straightforward, once you know how to get at the problem. Broken sash cords in a sliding sash window, for example, can be replaced; the cords of a faulty Venetian blind can be rethreaded; the hinges of a sagging door can be retightened. You can cure more serious ailments with tricks handed down through generations of carpenters. If necessary, you can strengthen a weak corner joint in a window sash with a "false tenon", or cut out a rotten patch in a timber sill and fit a specially shaped replacement section; somewhat more simply, you can adjust the parts of a window frame to free a sticking sash, reposition a doorstop to allow a warped door to close, or cut a replacement curved pane of glass *(opposite)* for an exotic window.

The appearance and performance of many old doors and windows can often be improved by such simple measures as a new coat of paint or wood stain, or the installation of draught-excluders and weatherstripping seals; some doors and windows, however, are so rotted, warped or irredeemably shabby as to be beyond repair. The simplest remedy in this case is to replace them with modern prefabricated units that come complete with finish frames and built-in weatherstripping. If the old door or window is a standard size, you can remove it and fasten a new one into the same rough opening in a matter of a few hours, without altering the structure of the wall. If you decide to install a larger unit, however—a sliding glass double door in place of a single wooden door, for example—you will have to shore up the walls and joists with temporary bracing, enlarge the hole in the wall and install a lintel above the opening—a procedure described in Chapter 2 of this book.

Why Windows Stick—and How to Free Them

Like the walls of a house, windows must withstand rain, snow, wind and sun. But walls are solid, permanent barriers built with weather-resistant materials; a movable window, however, is a relatively fragile machine, fitted with devices such as pulleys and weights or hinges and stays to make it open and close. Like all machines, windows at times move reluctantly and occasionally refuse to budge at all.

The basic parts of a window are almost always the same. It has glazed sashes that slide or swing open, a frame, and narrow strips at the sides and top of the frame to hold the sash in place. But each type of window has a different mechanism and a few special parts, and in each type the parts fit together in a different fashion and serve slightly different functions.

The commonest type of window in older houses is the vertical sliding sash window *(opposite page, above)* which originated in the late 17th century and became a standard feature in most houses built between 1700 and 1900. As well as its aesthetic virtues—which blended harmoniously with the developing architectural styles during this period—this window design also has considerable practical advantages: it takes up no extra space when it is open, and it allows stale air to be drawn out of the top of the window at the same time as fresh air enters at the bottom. But, because of the number of moving parts it has, and the ease with which the channels can become blocked, the vertical sliding sash window is more prone than most other designs to sticking and jamming.

The most common cause of jammed sashes is paint that has dried while the window is closed, sealing the gaps between the sashes and the staff beads. The sashes can usually be freed by breaking the paint seal and prising with a putty knife, an old screwdriver or a crowbar *(page 10)*. If the sashes still refuse to move freely, the channels are probably blocked by a layer of old paint and dirt. This layer can be removed with a scraper and sandpaper *(page 11, above)*, although in some stubborn cases you may have to remove the sash completely *(pages 14–15)* to do a thorough job. If the sash sticks in a window with clean channels, slip a piece of paper along the joints between the staff beads and the sash, to see whether the sash is binding there. Once you find the point of friction, you may be able to free the sash by knocking the bead with a wooden block and hammer *(page 11, below)*. If this does not work, remove the bead *(page 14)*, move it back slightly and renail it to the inner lining—be sure to move the bead only a fraction, or the sash will rattle in the wind. Do not try to use the easy trick of removing the sash and planing down its sides—however little wood you shave away, you will almost certainly end up with a rattling sash.

A sash that will not open fully for none of the above reasons, or that will not stay open at all, usually indicates that the mechanism is at fault. You can repair an older vertical sash window whose weight is counterbalanced by a pulley and a weight by simply replacing a cord *(pages 14–15)*. In newer sash windows, the counterbalance may be a type of spiral balance that generally cannot be repaired and must be replaced if faulty.

On both sliding sashes and non-rebated casement sashes, corners that have worked loose can be repaired by chiselling out the existing tenon and replacing it with a new section known as a "false tenon" *(page 12)*. L-shaped bars screwed to a corner to strengthen a joint rarely provide an effective repair, because the screws will not grip securely in unsound timber. If the upper sash of a sliding window does not meet the top rail evenly when closed, cut a thin timber fillet that will fill the gap and then glue or screw it to the rail.

Casement windows, which are now installed almost universally in new houses, consist in their simplest form of a single sash attached to a frame with hinges, but designs vary widely to accommodate different numbers and sizes of fixed lights and opening sashes *(opposite page, below)*. The sashes may be hinged on one side or along the top, or they may be hung on pivot hinges on both sides or on the top and bottom rails. Standard sashes close flush with the window frame, but storm-proof windows have rebated sashes that project beyond the frame.

Because timber casement sashes are attached to the frame in the same way as doors are hung on their linings or frames, they are prone to many of the same faults and often require similar repairs. To correct a sagging sash, the hinges can be shimmed out or reset in wooden plugs *(page 20)*. If a double-glazed sash is sagging, the cause is often incorrect or insufficient wedging of the glass in the sash rebate; in this case, you will have to take out the glass and position setting blocks according to the required pattern as shown on page 75. A warped sash that will not close tightly against the frame can sometimes be corrected by repositioning the stay nearer to the closing side, but if this remedy is not sufficient you will have to scribe and plane the frame as you would for a door *(page 21)*.

Windows made of metal or plastic are more weather-resistant than those made of timber and are less likely to need repair. Steel windows that stick because of corrosion should be cleaned of all rust and then primed and repainted *(page 44)*. Modern windows that are made with aluminium and plastic (uPVC) require very little maintenance *(pages 76–77)*.

A vertical sliding sash window. The frame consists of two pulley stiles, a head and a sill. Sliding inside the pulley stiles are an inner and an outer sash, which are held by three vertical strips on each side: a staff bead on the inside, a parting bead between the sashes, and a projecting strip of outer lining. Each sash frame is made up of vertical stiles and horizontal rails, and is often divided by glazing bars that secure individual panes of glass. The pulleys, cords and weights that counterbalance the sashes are boxed in on both sides of the frame by three pieces of lining and are separated by a pocket parting or "feather".

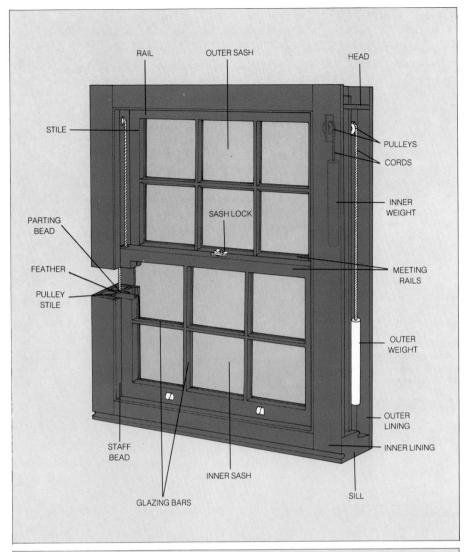

A storm-proof casement window. The basic frame of jambs, head and sill is divided by a vertical mullion and a horizontal transom into three sections: a top-hung fanlight, a fixed light and a side-hung sash. Each opening sash consists of a frame of rails and stiles that is often divided into separate panes by glazing bars. The side-hung sash and fanlight can be secured in an open position with casement stays; the side-hung sash is locked in its closed position by a fastener. Rebates on the rails and stiles of the fanlight and opening sash seal out draughts. A drip moulding along the exterior of the frame head deflects rainwater, and a drip groove along the underside of the sill prevents water penetrating the wall or sub-sill.

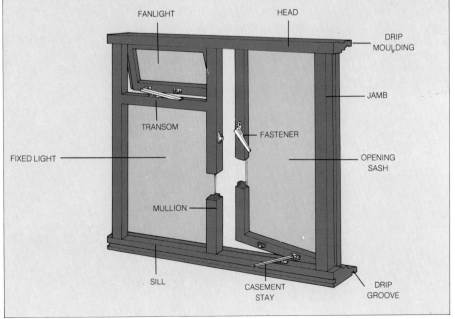

Freeing a Jammed Sash

Breaking a paint seal. Force a wide-bladed putty knife into the joint between one side of the sash and the staff bead. Work the knife round both sides of the sash, then force it into the joint between the bottom of the sash and the staff bead. If the sash still will not move, go outside the house and check the joint between the outside of the sash and the parting bead; repeat the procedure there if necessary.

Loosening the channels. Force the blade of a heavy screwdriver between the sash and the pulley stile; if the sash has a groove for a sash cord, use it as the point of entry for the blade. Prise the sash away from the stile, then repeat the procedure at the other side of the sash. Continue to work the sash to the right and left until you can slide it open.

Prising the sash up from outside. If all else fails, go outside the house and wedge a crowbar between the window sill and the sash. Set a block of wood on the sill under the crowbar for leverage and prise the sash up, working first under the corners of the sash.

Easing a Tight Sash

Cleaning the channels. On the inside of a wooden channel, use a scraper or triangular shave hook to scrape off loose paint and debris. Clean the pulley stiles first, then the sides of the staff beads, parting beads and outer linings. Smooth the cleaned channels by rubbing with sandpaper.

Lubricating the channels. A block of beeswax run up and down the channels three or four times will apply a light coat of wax to the pulley stiles and the sides of the beads and outer lining. But if you intend to paint the window, be sure to do that job first, before you wax the channels. Silicone spray lubricant can also be applied to timber parts, and it is better than wax as a lubricant for metal or plastic window parts.

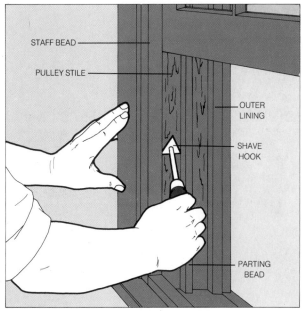

STAFF BEAD

PULLEY STILE

OUTER LINING

SHAVE HOOK

PARTING BEAD

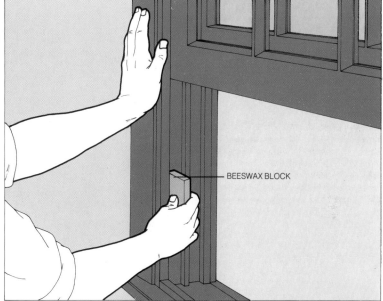

BEESWAX BLOCK

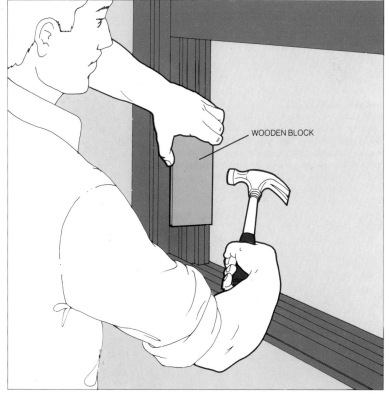

WOODEN BLOCK

Straightening bowed staff beads. If a sash binds against a staff bead, set a wooden block against the side of the bead where it sticks and tap it gently with a hammer several times. Take care not to displace the bead from the pulley stile. If the bead cannot be straightened by this method, prise it off with a chisel blade, reposition it so that the sash will slide freely and then renail it to the pulley stile.

Repairing a Loose Corner: Fitting a False Tenon

1 Marking the corner. Remove the sash from the window by unscrewing the hinges. To avoid cracking the glass pane, chip away putty and remove the glass *(page 35)*. Secure the sash in a vice with the loose rail upwards. Measuring from the end of the stile, mark off the width of the rail less the width of the rebate, then use a combination square to draw a pencil line across the stile at this distance from the end. In the same way, mark across the rail the width of the stile plus about 20 mm *(right)*. Using a mortise gauge set to the thickness of the existing tenon and centred on the sash, score along both rail and stile up to the marked lines.

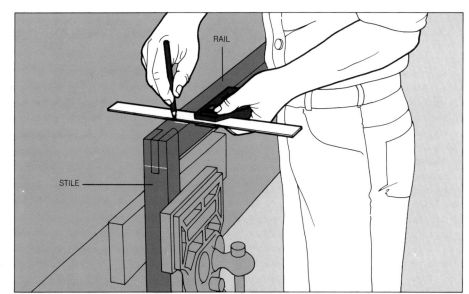

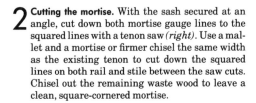

2 Cutting the mortise. With the sash secured at an angle, cut down both mortise gauge lines to the squared lines with a tenon saw *(right)*. Use a mallet and a mortise or firmer chisel the same width as the existing tenon to cut down the squared lines on both rail and stile between the saw cuts. Chisel out the remaining waste wood to leave a clean, square-cornered mortise.

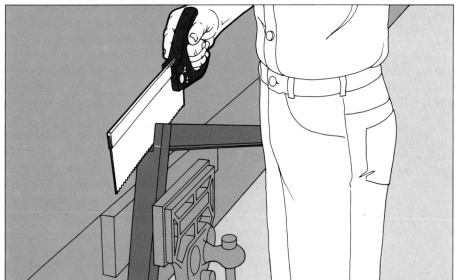

3 Inserting the false tenon. Cut a tenon from scrap timber slightly longer and wider than the new mortise. Apply waterproof glue to both sides of the tenon and the two edges that will be concealed, then slot the tenon into the mortise and wipe off excess glue. When the glue has set, plane the exposed edges of the false tenon flush with the rail and the stile. Reglaze the sash and secure it to the frame.

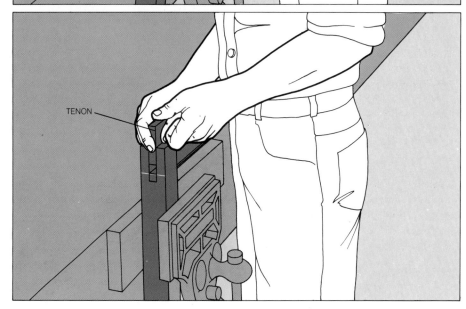

The Age-Old Language of Doors and Windows

Muntin and *mullion*, *transom* and *kerf*—the words sound like a witch's chant. In fact, these haunting terms stand for ordinary objects: the parts of a door or a window, and the joints and cuts that fit the parts together.

The ancient craft of joinery—that is, fine carpentry, such as that needed in constructing doors and windows—has evolved over the years, but much of its basic vocabulary remains essentially unchanged. Like the language of any skilled craft, the words in the following list are worth knowing for their economy and precision; properly understood, they tell you exactly what piece or cut is involved. And the derivations of some of the words yield fascinating glimpses into history.

APRON: An inside moulding that lies against the wall beneath the window board. It hangs like an apron over the joint between window board and wall.

ARCHITRAVE: The timber moulding used to cover the joint between the top and sides of a door lining or window frame and the surrounding wall surface.

FANLIGHT: A fixed or opening window above a door or larger casement window.

FLASHING: A piece of metal—or other material that is impervious to water—that weatherproofs the joint between a roof covering and another structure such as a dormer window.

GLAZING BAR: A vertical or horizontal bar that divides a window sash or frame into separate panes of glass. It is also called an "astragal"—from the Greek word for ankle bone.

HEADER: Timber lintel over window or door in a load-bearing timber frame wall.

JAMB: A piece at the side of the frame round a window or door, adjoining the moving parts. The word comes from the Latin *gamba*, meaning leg—the jambs are legs that straddle the opening.

KERF: The cut made by a saw blade. The word comes almost unchanged from the Old English word *cyrf*, which means cut.

LIGHT: A window, a section of a divided window, or a pane set in a window. A "fixed light" is a window or section of a window that does not open.

LINTEL: A beam of concrete, steel or timber across the top of a door or window, supporting the weight of the wall above.

MEETING RAILS: In a sliding sash window, the top rail of the bottom sash and the bottom rail of the top sash. The two rails touch when the window is closed.

MITRE: An angle cut into an edge to make it fit a matching angle in another piece; the ends of many mouldings are cut at 45-degree angles to form right-angles.

MORTISE: A recess cut in one piece to hold another. A shallow mortise is often fitted with hardware, such as a hinge; a deep one holds a tenon, forming a mortise and tenon joint.

MULLION: A slender vertical bar separating adjoining sashes or fixed lights in a window. The original Latin word meant in the middle.

MUNTIN: A vertical strip separating the panels of a door.

PARTING BEAD: A narrow strip of moulding separating the moving sashes of a window or panels of a patio door.

PULLEY STILE: In the frame of a sliding sash window, one of the two vertical boards adjacent to the sashes in which the pulleys for the cords are fixed.

RAIL: The horizontal top or bottom piece of a door or a window sash.

REBATE: A step cut in the edge of a board, to form a joint with another board similarly cut or to hold in place thin sheet material, such as glass. The word comes from the Old French, *rabattre*, meaning to beat down or deduct.

SASH: The opening part of any window; from the French *chassis*, meaning framework. As the word evolved in English, its pronunciation changed from *shasses* to *shases* to *sashes* to *sash*.

SASH CORD: One of four cords in a vertical sliding sash window by which the sashes are attached to their counterbalancing weights.

SEALED UNIT: A double glazing unit consisting of two panes of glass separated by a hermetically sealed air gap.

SECONDARY GLAZING: A pane of glass or clear plastic fixed to the sash or frame of a single-glazed window.

SETTING BLOCK: A small block of wood or plastic placed in the rebate of a window frame or sash to centre and support a large pane of glass or a sealed unit.

SHIM: A thin, wedge-shaped piece inserted under or between other pieces to adjust their position.

SILL: The horizontal piece at the bottom of a window frame, generally slanted down towards the outside of the house to shed water. The inside, shelf-like piece commonly mislabelled the sill is properly called the window board.

STAFF BEAD: In a sliding sash window, a narrow strip of moulding round the inside of the frame that holds the inner sash in its channel.

STILE: A vertical side piece of a door or a window sash; from the Dutch *stijl*, meaning doorpost.

THRESHOLD: A strip fastened to the floor beneath a door; a doorsill. The word derives from the original meaning of *thresh*, to trample or tread.

TRANSOM: A horizontal bar separating adjoining fixed lights or sashes in a window, or separating a door from a fanlight.

WEEPHOLE: A small drainage hole in the sill of a window frame through which condensation water can escape.

Replacing a Broken Sash Cord

Without some kind of support, the sashes of a vertical sliding window would drop to the bottom of the window frame every time you raised them. The traditional support method, standard from the late 17th century up to about 1900, uses a system of counterweights much like those of a lift or a dumb-waiter. Two pulleys, one for each sash, are built into the top of each vertical pulley stile; from the sides of the sashes, cords run over the pulleys to metal or masonry weights hidden behind the pulley stiles *(right and page 9)*. This simple, reliable system has only one drawback: eventually a cord breaks and the sash then jams in its channel or else falls to the bottom of the window frame.

To replace a cord of the lower sash, generally the first to break, you must remove the staff beads that hold the sash in place, the sash, the parting beads that separate the two sashes, and the pocket piece that covers the sash weight inside the pulley stile. Next, you must thread a new cord over the pulley and attach it to the sash and weight. While you have the sash out, it is a good idea to replace the unbroken cord. At the same time, check the cords of the other sash for wear; you may avoid trouble later by replacing them as well. To get at the upper sash cords, you must first take out the lower sash and the parting beads.

You can replace the broken cord with a length of new waxed sash cord—do not use ordinary rope, which wears too quickly. Sash cord is sold in several thicknesses, depending on the weight it has to hold. To ensure that you buy the correct strength for your window, take a piece of the old cord with you to the hardware shop.

Sash weights are occasionally involved in seemingly unrelated window problems. Long nails driven through the inner lining or pulley stile can interfere with the weights, jamming the sash or leaving it unsupported; remove these nails using pincers *(page 23)*. If sash cords stretch, so that the weights lie on the bottom of the window frame, a sash will not stay fully open. You need not replace a stretched cord; simply remove the sash and pocket piece, cut a few centimetres from the end of the cord, then retie it to the weight.

1 **Removing the lower sash.** Prise off the staff beads. To avoid damaging the inside of the frame, lean through the open window and push a chisel blade between a staff bead and the inner lining from the outside; if necessary tap gently with a mallet. Remove the nails from the beads with pincers. Raise the sash slightly, angle it towards you and lift it out of the frame *(below)*. Holding the unbroken cord on the opposite side of the sash, cut the cord near the sash and lower the weight gently to the bottom of the pulley stile. Rest the sash on the window board and mark the side of the sash where the old cord ends. Measure from the bottom of the sash to this mark; transfer that measurement from the bottom of the window board to a point above it on the pulley stile. Pull the cords and retaining nails out of their grooves.

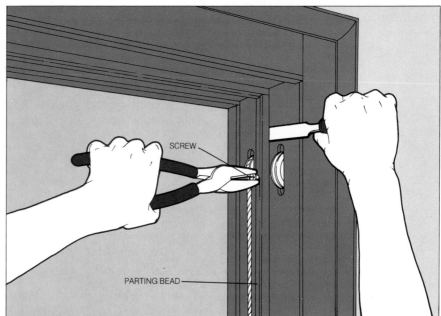

2 **Pulling out the parting beads.** Lower the upper sash and pull out the parting bead using pincers. If it is stuck, drill a pilot hole in the parting bead on one side of the window about 73 mm from the top and thread a short wood screw into it. Caution: do not run the screw right through the bead and into the pulley stile. Pull steadily on the screw with a pair of pliers until you can slip a wood chisel behind the end of the parting bead. From this point, prise the bead out a little at a time with the wood chisel, moving the chisel downwards as the gap widens between the stile and the parting bead. When the top half of the bead is free, slide the sash to the top of the window frame, then continue to prise out the lower half of the parting bead. Pull out the parting bead on the other side of the window frame in the same way.

STRING

NEW CORD

NAIL

3 **Taking out the pocket pieces.** Remove the screws in one of the pocket pieces and prise it out of the pulley stiles using a wood chisel. Reach into the pocket, take out the sash weight and untie the broken cord. If the pocket piece is concealed by paint, rap on the lower part of the pulley stile with a hammer until the outline of the pocket piece appears and cut round it using a trimming knife. Remove the pocket piece on the other side of the window frame in the same way.

4 **Putting in the new cords.** Tie a bent nail to a piece of string, tie the other end of the string to one end of a new sash cord, and feed the string over the pulley until the nail appears at the pocket; then pull the cord over the pulley and down to the pocket. Untie the string and tie the cord to the sash weight with a double knot, leaving about 75 mm of surplus cord. Thread a cord over the opposite pulley in the same way.

POCKET PIECE

WEIGHT

5 **Attaching the new cords to the sash.** Pull down on one of the new cords to raise the sash weight; when it touches the pulley, slacken the cord to lower the weight about 50 mm and pin the cord to the pulley stile. Cut the cord level with the mark on the pulley stile that you made in Step 1. Rest the sash on the window board. Place the cord in the groove on one side of the sash, with the end of the cord touching the mark. Secure the cord in position with three 19 mm broad-head galvanized nails; keep the top nail well below the top of the sash so that it will be clear of the pulley. Remove the nail pinning the cord to the pulley stile. Attach the other cord in the same way. Replace the pocket pieces, parting beads, sash and staff beads, using short nails that will not reach the sash weights. Do not drive any nails into either of the pocket pieces.

Fine Work on Treasured Windows

A window sash in a traditional vertical sliding sash window is an interlocking grid of wood holding small panes of glass. Vertical stiles and horizontal rails form the sturdy outer framework of the sash; relatively fragile strips called glazing bars support the panes within. All of these timber pieces are snugly jointed with interlocking notches and projections called mortises and tenons. To preserve the beauty of a valuable or antique window, it is better to replace individual parts, when necessary, than to substitute an entire modern sash.

Replacing a glazing bar—the piece most likely to be damaged when a window is broken—is an especially intricate job. To replace the bars that extend right across the sash—in the sash shown below, the vertical bars—you must take the whole sash apart. To replace one of the shorter bars, either dismantle the sash or use the shortcut method described opposite. With both methods, however, you must first take the sash out of the window and carefully remove all the glass, keeping each pane intact for reinstallation.

To ensure a proper fit, always get a new glazing bar of the same design as the one you are replacing. Most window frame manufacturers stock a variety of designs; if you cannot match your own, you can have one specially milled. The wooden pins that in some sashes lock the glazing bar tenons into the mortises can be easily shaped by hand from scrap timber, or steel pins are available from hardware shops.

Not all glazing bars are individually fitted together. If the one you must replace is part of a decorative one-piece grille fitted over a single pane of glass, a window frame manufacturer should be able to supply you with a timber or plastic replacement. These grilles, which generally come with instructions, are simply snapped in place.

The intricate joinery of a sash. In this traditional window sash, the ends of horizontal rails are shaped into projections (called tenons), which fit into holes (called mortises) cut into the ends of the vertical stiles. Each of these mortise and tenon joints is secured by a wooden or steel pin driven completely through it. The interior wood strips, called glazing bars, are also joined with mortises and tenons. The tenons of the vertical bars fit into mortises in the rails. Horizontal glazing bars have tenons that fit into mortises in the vertical bars and the stiles.

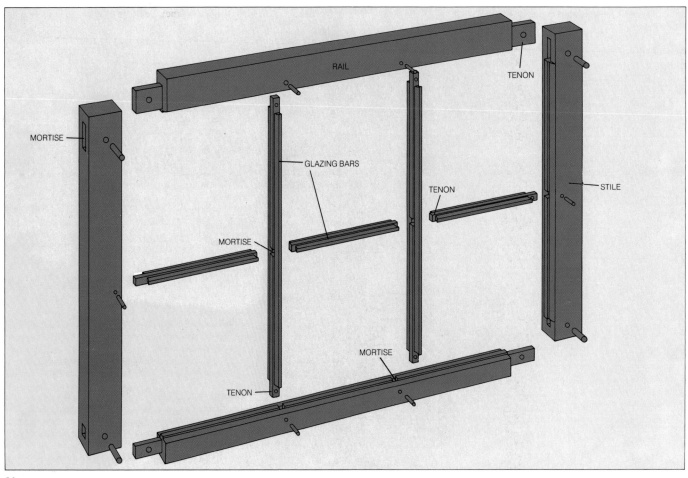

Splicing a Short Bar

1 **Removing the pin.** Take the sash out of the window *(pages 14–15)*. Chip away putty and extract glazing sprigs *(page 35, Steps 2 and 3)*, then remove the panes of glass. Set the sash on offcuts of timber. If the damaged glazing bar fits into a stile, scrape the paint and putty from the pin in the bar's mortise and tenon joint, then drive the pin completely out of the hole with a nail punch, a blunted nail or—best of all—with a wooden dowel of the same shape and diameter as the pin. Cut the damaged bar in half, pull its tenons out of the mortises and set the pieces aside. Cut a new glazing bar 3 mm longer than the combined length of the two pieces you have removed.

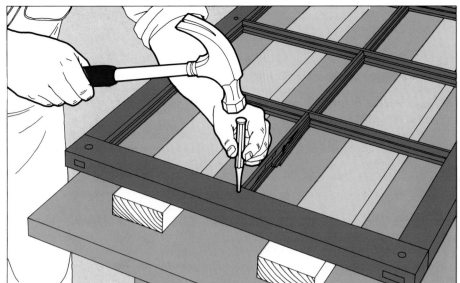

2 **Shaping the new glazing bar.** Judging by eye and using the old glazing bar as a guide, mark the shape of the tenons on the new bar and use a coping saw to cut the ends of the new bar to the desired shape of the tenons.

3 **Fitting the new glazing bar.** Make a diagonal cut through the centre of the new bar and taper the ends of the tenons slightly to ease their fit; then coat the diagonal surfaces with waterproof PVA glue, insert the tenons into the mortises, and clamp the two pieces of the bar together for at least 12 hours *(inset)*.

If the glazing bar is one that fits into a stile, drill through the pinholes of the stile to make a hole in the new tenon. Coat a pin with glue and gently tap it into place with a mallet.

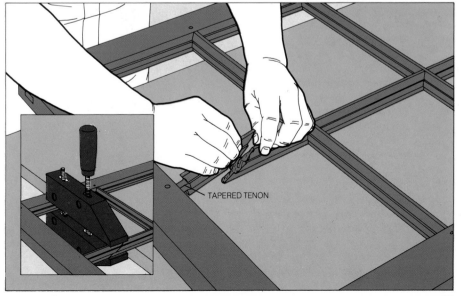

TAPERED TENON

Simple Carpentry for Everyday Door Problems

The vast majority of doors are made of timber and are categorized as either "flush" or "panel" (below, right). An internal door is hung on a lining that covers the whole thickness of the wall, and closes against planted rebate stops that are nailed or screwed to the top and sides of the lining; an external door is hung on a frame which is narrower than the wall thickness and which has an integral rebate that acts as the doorstop. Although a door that has been correctly installed will withstand years of continual use, wear and tear take their inevitable toll—and few working parts of a house cause more frustration than a door that rattles, sticks or refuses to lock, or even to close at all.

A rattling door can usually be cured by filing the keep plate (page 20, below), then enlarging the recess in the jamb with a chisel to align with the filed edge of the plate. Alternatively, if the door stop consists of a strip of wood nailed to the lining (known as a "planted rebate"), prise the stop from the jamb (page 23) and renail it up against the closed door.

A sagging or sticking door calls for a more careful diagnosis. First, check the hinges; the screws that anchor the hinge leaves to the jamb may have pulled loose. If the screws turn but will not tighten, the screwholes in the jamb have become enlarged. In that case, fill the holes with wooden plugs and replace the screws (page 20, top left). Do not attempt to replace loose screws with screws of a larger diameter, because the new screw heads would be too large to fit the existing countersunk holes in the hinge leaf.

An easy remedy for a door that binds along the jamb at the top of its closing side is to shim out the bottom hinge with cardboard (page 20, top right). Similarly, for a door that binds towards the bottom of the lock side, shim the upper hinge.

Paint build-up, too, can prevent a door from moving freely. To pinpoint trouble spots, insert a piece of thin cardboard along the joint between the closed door and the lining. Wherever the door pinches or presses the cardboard, remove the paint with a scraper and sandpaper.

More serious is a warped door. If the door moves freely but will not stay closed, check to be sure that the latch enters the opening in the keep plate when the door is shut. If

the latch and the keep plate opening are out of alignment by only a few millimetres, file the keep plate as for a rattling door. A larger misalignment can sometimes be cured by repositioning the keep plate over an enlarged recess. Usually, however, the solution for a badly warped door that hits the door stop before the latch can engage with the keep plate is to adjust the door stop. A planted rebate stop should be carefully prised from the jamb and then repositioned to follow the contour of the door. However, if the stop consists of a rebate in the jamb, you will have to plane the rebate to fit (page 21).

A plane is a versatile tool for many door repairs and installation procedures. A smoothing plane (opposite page, above) can be used to plane the edges of a door; alternatively, use a jack plane—which is essen-

tially a longer version of the smoothing plane—for the long side edges, and a block plane, which can be held in one hand, for the short edges. For the rebates on a door lining, use a rebate plane (opposite page, below), which has a cutting iron that extends across its whole width.

If you are planing a door on its hinges, wedge the door firmly open to leave both hands free for planing. If you must plane the long hinge side of a door, support the door by securing it in a door jack (page 103) or in a slot cut into a sawhorse top butted firmly against a wall. When planing, work with the grain and always try to remove the wood in several thin shavings. Apply pressure to the toe, or front, of the plane at the beginning of each stroke, then gradually shift the pressure to the heel, or back, as you finish the cut.

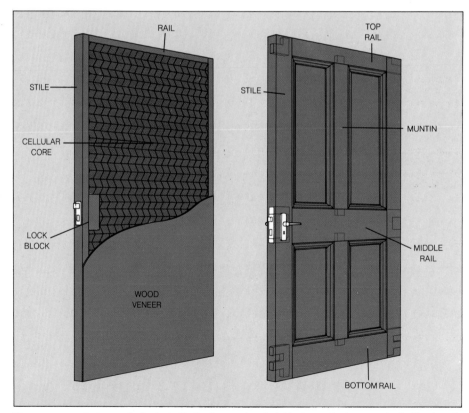

The anatomy of doors. A typical flush door (above, left) consists of a frame of horizontal rails and vertical stiles enclosing a cellular core of paperboard, extruded chipboard or a similar material. The sides are faced with thin wood veneer; the hinge and closing edges may be protected with lipping. The latch and lock casing is housed in a lock block attached to a vertical stile. A traditional panel door (above, right) features plain or moulded panels held in grooves or rebates along the edges of the vertical stiles and muntins and the horizontal rails. The stiles and rails are joined with haunched mortise and tenon joints, or dowelled joints on more modern doors.

Planes for Doors

Anatomy of a smoothing plane. The iron and cap iron of a smoothing plane are fastened together with a cap screw to form a double iron, which rests on a slanting piece called the frog. The lever cap and its cam fasten the double iron in place; locking pressure is adjusted by turning the lever-cap screw. On the sole of the plane, the mouth opening through which the iron projects is adjusted by loosening two frog-bed screws and by turning a frog-adjusting screw; move the frog forwards for fine work and back for coarse.

The cap iron, which deflects and breaks up the planed-off wood, may also be adjusted. Set it about 1.5 mm behind the cutting edge of the iron for all-purpose planing; move it closer for fine jobs. The adjusting nut controls the depth of the cut the iron makes, and the adjusting lever aligns the iron's cutting edge. A knob and a handle mounted on the sole provide holds for two hands.

Anatomy of a rebate plane. The full-width iron of a rebate plane enables it to cut or smooth right-angled rebates. The iron is held in place by the lever cap and its screw; the depth of the iron can be adjusted by easing the lever cap knurled screw and then turning the adjusting screw. When the plane is used to cut a new rebate, the detachable parallel fence and the depth stop (on the far side of the plane) are set to the required width and depth. The iron and lever cap are moved to the forward position in order to plane into a corner.

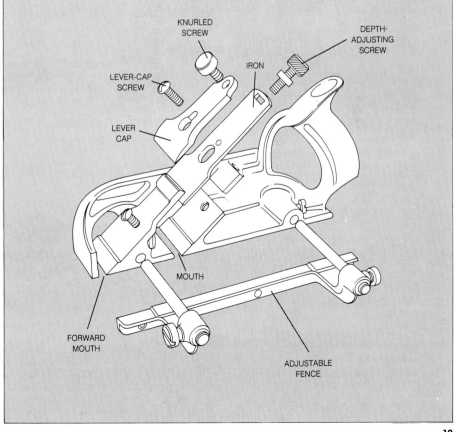

Resetting Hinges and Plates

Tightening loose screws. Unscrew both hinges from the jamb and remove the door. Cut plugs of wood to the size of the hinge screwholes, coat the plugs with glue and tap them into the holes. Let the glue set, then drill pilot holes through the plugs and screw the hinges back in place.

Shimming a hinge. Wedge the door open, loosen the screws that fasten a hinge leaf to the jamb and insert a cardboard shim, slotted at the level of the screws, behind the hinge leaf. Add a second shim if necessary.

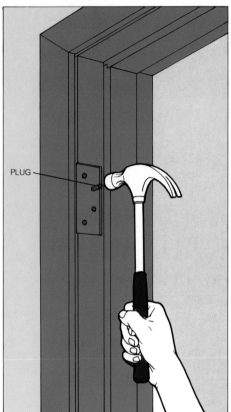

PLUG

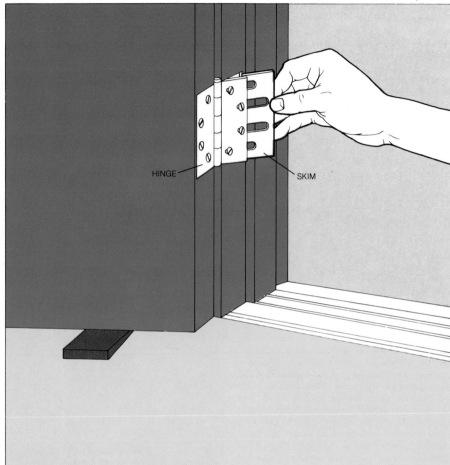

HINGE   SKIM

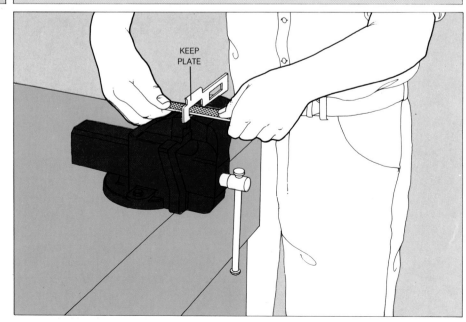

KEEP
PLATE

Filing a keep plate. If an ordinary keep plate is less than 5 mm out of alignment with the door latch, unscrew the plate from the jamb and enlarge the plate opening with a flat double-cut file. Remove 1.5 mm of metal at a time until the latch fits. Enlarge the keep plate hole in the jamb with a chisel if necessary.

Shaving a Door to Fit

Trimming the edges. If a door sticks at the top, wedge it half way open and use a smoothing plane to trim the top. Plane until there is a clearance of 3 mm between the top of the door and the lining head. If a door sticks along its hinge side and the problem cannot be cured by shimming the hinges, unscrew the hinge leaves from the lining, then remove the hinges from the door and support the door securely with its hinge edge upwards. Use a smoothing or jack plane to plane the hinge edge to fit the lining. Chisel out the hinge recesses to the correct depth *(pages 102–103)* and rehang the door.

Planing a Rebate for a Warped Door

1 **Scribing the rebate.** Get a helper to hold the door with its closing face just touching the rebate stop and its latch withheld—do not force the door against the rebate until the latch engages with the keep plate. Measure the widest gap between the rebate and the closing face of the door—this will usually be at the bottom or, as here, at the top—and cut a small block of scrap wood to this thickness. Hold the point of a pencil against this block and, keeping the block butted against the door, push the block along the entire length of the frame to mark a line on the rebate *(inset)*.

PENCIL LINE

WOODEN BLOCK

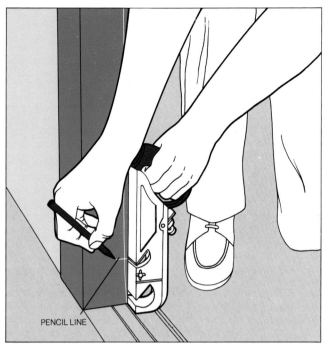

PENCIL LINE

2 **Chiselling the rebate end.** At the end of the rebate from which waste must be cut—in this case, the bottom end—hold a rebate plane against the rebate with its front end butted into the corner. A few millimetres farther from the end of the rebate than the plane's cutting iron, mark a horizontal line across the rebate to meet the vertical scribed line. Use a wood chisel and mallet to remove the waste area between the horizontal line and the vertical scribed line.

3 **Planing the rebate.** Using a rebate plane, carefully plane the rebate down to the pencil line. Keep the side of the plane butted firmly against the jamb, so that the iron cuts evenly across the entire width of the rebate. Sand the rebate smooth, then prime and paint or varnish the planed face to match the existing decoration.

PENCIL LINE

Working on the Architraves and Stops

The architraves that are fixed round both doors and windows serve to bridge the gap between the lining or frame and the exposed edges of the inside wall. The stops or rebates keep a door or the sash of a casement window from swinging too far through the opening, and also help to seal the gaps between the door or window and the lining that encloses it on three sides.

On an internal door, the stops may be either planted rebates—that is, strips of timber that are fixed on to a plain lining or frame—or integral rebates that form part of the lining or frame itself. The more intricate the moulding of both architraves and stops, the more likely they are to be accidentally defaced by knocks or scratches or to lose their sharp profiles because of overpainting. The following pages describe how to remove old architraves and planted stops and install new ones; although the illustrations show the work being carried out on a door, the instructions apply generally to both doors and windows.

Your timber merchant will stock lengths of moulding for architraves and stops in a wide variety of shapes, thicknesses and widths. Alternatively, you can have the piece cut specially at a mill; however, this custom work will be expensive because it may entail the shaping of a special blade to cut your pattern.

Architraves are usually set back about 5 mm from the inside edge of the lining; so long as the architrave overlaps the lining sufficiently for nailing purposes, however, the distance it is set back can be varied according to personal taste.

Where two pieces of architrave meet, the ends of each piece are mitred to make a joint. The top piece of architrave has two 45-degree mitre cuts, fitting similar cuts at the tops of the two side pieces to form right-angled joints. Some windows without projecting window boards are cased like picture frames, with four casing strips mitre-cut to 45-degree angles at the ends.

At joints between moulded stops that have shaped profiles, the two side stops are scribed and coped to fit the contour of the head stop (page 27, Step 2); this produces a joint that will not separate as easily as a mitred one. Plain stops that are rectangular or square in cross-section are joined together with simple butt joints.

Both architraves and stops should be nailed with special care. Drive in each nail until the nail head alone projects above the wood surface, then carefully complete the job with a nail punch. When nailing the side architraves on to a door lining, do not drive any nails in at the location of the keep plate (pages 106–107).

Removing Architraves and Stops

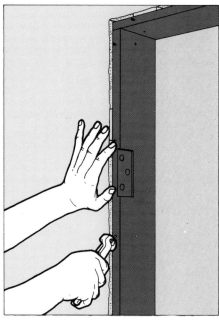

Pulling out the stops. Score the joints between the stop and the jamb with a scraper or putty knife, then, starting at the bottom of a side stop, set a chisel between stop and lining, with the bevel of the chisel against the lining. Tapping the chisel with a mallet, work up the stop to prise it away from the lining. Repeat the procedure on the other side stop, then on the head stop.

Prising off the architrave. Take the architrave part of the way off with a chisel, as for a stop, then insert the flat end of a crowbar behind the outer edge of the architrave. Place a scrap of wood behind the bar to avoid marring the wall. Slowly prise the architrave free, working up from the bottom. Remove the other side architrave and the head architrave in the same way.

Extracting nails. If a nail does not come out with the architrave but remains behind in the lining or wall, grip the head with pincers and roll the head of the pincers against the wall to twist the nail free. If the nail is in a stop or architrave that you plan to re-use, grip the shank of the nail protruding at the back and pull the head end completely through the piece.

Cutting New Architraves

1 Measuring the head architrave. Use a combination square to mark at several points the desired set-back of the architrave—usually about 5 mm outside the inner edge of the lining. The marks for the top and side pieces of architrave should intersect at a precise corner point. Measure the distance between the jambs at the top, then add the amount of set-back on each side. Mark this distance on the inside edge of a piece of architrave that is long enough to leave sufficient room for the mitre cuts, which will fan outwards from the marks.

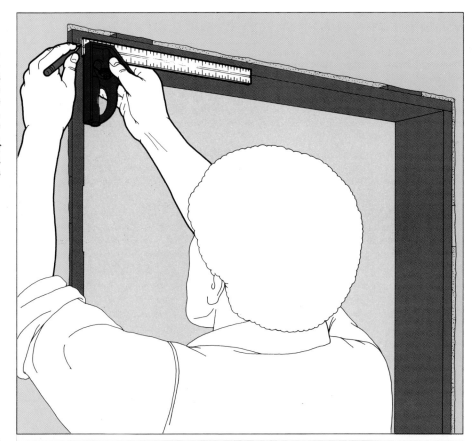

2 Cutting the mitres. In a mitre box firmly secured to a workbench, place the architrave flat side down, set the saw for a 45-degree cut outwards from the mark and, using long, even strokes, saw the strip just outside one of the marks you have made. Reverse the 45-degree angle and cut the second mitre just outside the mark at the other end of the architrave.

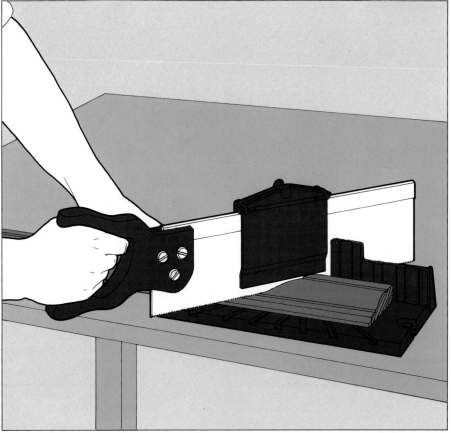

3 **Nailing the top architrave.** With a helper, set the narrow edge of the architrave at the marks on the lining, then tack the ends of the architrave to the lining head. Starting from one end, drive 37 mm oval nails through the bottom of the architrave into the lining, spacing the nails about 250 mm apart. If you are working on a timber-frame wall, also nail the top edge of the architrave into the cross stud behind the wall covering. Punch the nails and fill the holes.

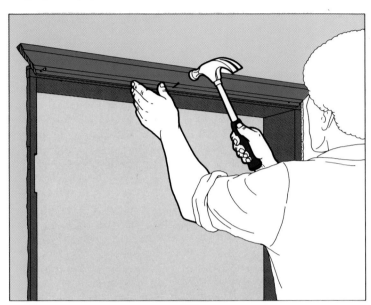

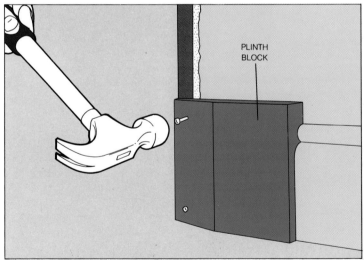

PLINTH BLOCK

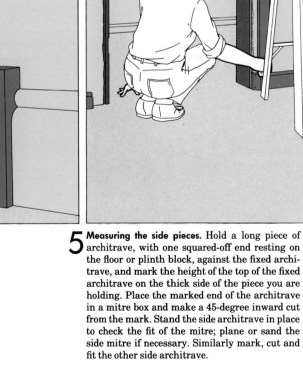

4 **Installing plinth blocks.** If you wish to install plinth blocks—decorative features that mediate between the different moulded profiles of a door architrave and the skirting boards—cut two pieces of wood of a type that matches the new architraves, slightly higher and thicker than the skirting boards. Attach the blocks on either side of the doorway with oval nails driven into the door lining, then toenail them to the skirting boards. Punch the nails beneath the surface and fill the holes.

5 **Measuring the side pieces.** Hold a long piece of architrave, with one squared-off end resting on the floor or plinth block, against the fixed architrave, and mark the height of the top of the fixed architrave on the thick side of the piece you are holding. Place the marked end of the architrave in a mitre box and make a 45-degree inward cut from the mark. Stand the side architrave in place to check the fit of the mitre; plane or sand the side mitre if necessary. Similarly mark, cut and fit the other side architrave.

6 **Attaching the side pieces.** With the mitred joint aligned, tack the side architrave in position against the set-back marks on the lining. Starting at the top, nail the inside edge of the architrave to the lining with 37 mm oval nails. On a timber-frame wall, also nail the outside edge of the architrave to the studs.

7 **Lock-nailing the joints.** About 25 mm from the outside corner of the architrave, drive one 37 mm oval nail vertically down through the top edge of the top architrave into the side architrave, and another horizontally through the edge of the side architrave and into the top architrave. The joint should now be even and tight.

Adding New Stops

1 **Nailing the head stop.** Measure between the sides of the lining and cut a length of stop moulding to fit. With the door closed and its latch held in the keep plate, hold the square edge of the stop moulding against the closing face of the door. Nail the head stop to the top of the lining with 25 mm oval nails spaced at intervals of about 250 mm. Punch the nails beneath the surface and fill the holes.

HEAD STOP

CLOSED DOOR

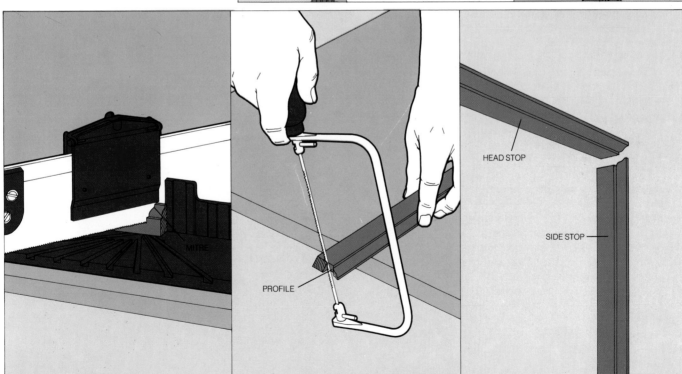

MITRE

PROFILE

HEAD STOP

SIDE STOP

2 **Coping the side stops.** Cut two lengths of stop moulding 25 mm longer than the distance from the lining head to the floor. Flat stops can be butted together; for mitred stops, cut a 45-degree mitre across the moulded face at the top end of each piece, angling from the moulded face to the flat face that fits against the jamb *(above, left)*. The cuts will leave a scalloped profile on each moulded face. Trace the profiles with a pencil and, following the marks, make a 90-degree cut through each piece with a coping saw *(above, centre)*. The ends of the coped pieces will fit snugly against the head stop *(above, right)*. Measure the lengths of the side stops, trim them at the bottom and hold them in position on the jambs with their square edges butted against the closed door. Nail the side stops as you did the head stop, then punch the nails and fill the holes.

The Base of a Window: Repairing Sills

The part of a window most vulnerable to damage and decay is the external sill, which is frequently bumped, banged and rained on. Rainwater that breaks through the painted or varnished surface of a timber sill *(right)* causes rot, which can very quickly spread to other parts of the frame; on concrete sills *(right, below)*, surface deterioration combined with frost can cause the sill to crack.

If a timber sill is just cracked or pitted, restoration is relatively straightforward. Remove all the paint, splinters and wood chips, using paint remover, putty knife and wire brush, then clean out the drip groove along the bottom of the sill with an old screwdriver blade or similar tool. Fill cracks and holes with wood filler and let it dry for the time specified by the manufacturer. Then prime and repaint the sill.

Rot is a more serious problem. If the entire sill is affected, the rot has probably spread and you will need to replace the whole frame. Where only a small area has been affected, the rot can be cut out and replaced with a section of new timber *(opposite page and overleaf)*. Hardwood is more resistant to rot but you can use either hardwood or softwood to match the existing timber. Where the rotten timber is at the front of the sill, mark and cut out a section that is wider at the back than at the front *(Steps 1 and 2)*, so that the replacement section will be wedged securely into the sound parts of the sill.

Surface deterioration or small areas of damage on a concrete sill must be chipped away with a bolster or cold chisel, and the sill renewed with fresh mortar *(page 31)*. A sill that has been structurally weakened by deep cracks requires more extensive chipping away and renewal; for this job you will have to construct and attach to the wall a timber box frame that will hold the mortar while it sets.

A projecting timber sill. A timber section that overhangs the wall is secured to the sill of the casement window frame with a tongue and groove joint. A U-shaped drip groove cut into the projecting part of the sill prevents rainwater from running back along the underside of the sill and penetrating the wall. Instead of the two-part sill which is illustrated here, some timber windows are fitted with a wide one-piece sill that projects beyond the wall.

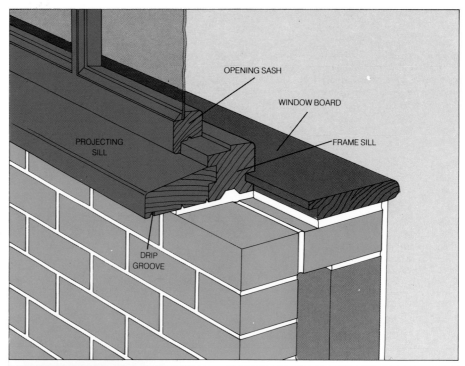

A composite sill. The timber sill that forms the bottom rail of the casement window frame rests on top of a concrete sill that projects over the edge of the wall. The upper surface of the concrete sill is sloping downwards so that rainwater can run off it. A galvanized steel water bar, which is securely bedded in mortar and held in special grooves along both the concrete and the timber sills, prevents any water from penetrating the joint between the two sills.

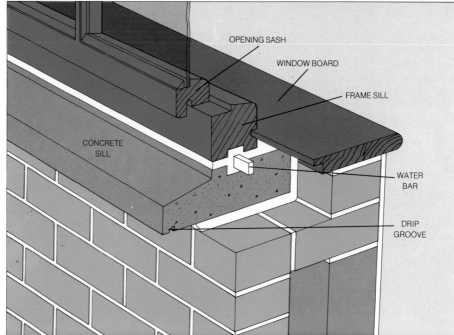

Replacing a Damaged Section in a Timber Sill

1 **Marking the sill.** Scrape off all loose paint from the sill with a scraper, then prod the sill with a screwdriver blade or other sharp instrument to find the extent of the damage—timber that feels soft or spongy is rotten and must be removed. About 50 mm on each side of the damaged area, draw a line from the front of the sill at an angle of about 45 degrees towards the back corner. At the back of the damaged area, join the two angled lines with a pencil line which runs parallel to the front of the sill.

2 **Cutting out the rot.** On the front of a sill that projects beyond the wall, use a tenon saw to cut along the angled lines up to the wall. On the part of the sill that is bedded on top of the wall or on a concrete sub-sill, use a mallet and wood chisel to chop out the damaged area: begin by chopping inside the marked lines to remove most of the waste, then cut back to the lines to leave smooth, even edges. Take care not to blunt the chisel by driving it into the wall or concrete sub-sill.

3 **Cutting the splice.** Measure the depth and length of the exposed area of sill, then add 2 mm to each dimension to allow for final adjustments to the splice. Using a marking gauge and a sliding bevel, transfer the measurements to a block of timber slightly thicker than the height of the cutaway portion of sill. Saw the timber to the marked dimensions, then plane as necessary until the splice fits snugly into the gap.

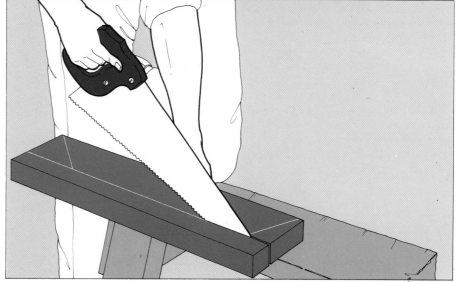

4 **Cutting the drip groove.** Mark two parallel lines on the underside of the timber splice, to join up with the existing drip grooves on the sound sections of the sill. Secure the splice, with the lines facing upwards, in a vice or with G-cramps. Use a hammer and chisel or a router to cut a groove between the marked lines to the same depth as the existing drip groove.

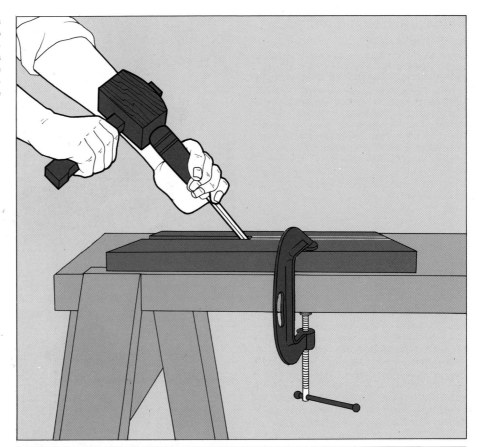

5 **Securing the splice.** Drill fixing holes through the front of the splice—about two holes for each 300 mm length—and countersink the holes. Spread waterproof woodworking glue along the back and angled sides of the splice, then fit the splice in position in the sill—tapping gently with a wooden mallet if necessary—and wipe off surplus glue. Secure the splice to the back of the sill with No. 10 brass, galvanized or sherardized screws of a suitable length; the screw should project beyond the splice and into the sill by about 25 mm. Fill the countersunk holes and any cracks in the sill with a wood filler. Plane the top of the splice flush with the surrounding sill using a smoothing plane. Finally, prime and then paint the entire sill.

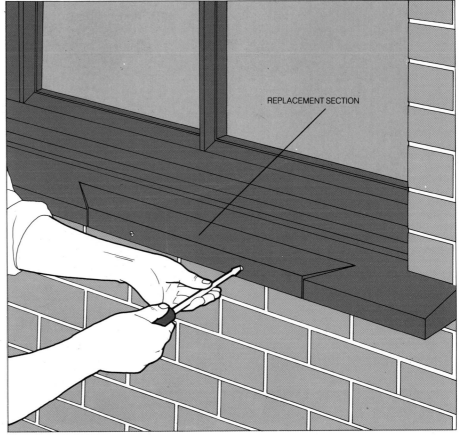

REPLACEMENT SECTION

Repairing a Concrete Sill

1 **Chipping off old concrete.** Chip away the crumbling surface or damaged area of the sill with a club hammer and cold chisel. Cut into the sound concrete to make as square an edge as possible and hack the exposed surface to provide a good key for the fresh mortar.

2 **Brushing on the slurry.** Mix cement with a bonding agent such as SBR (styrene butadiene rubber latex) according to the manufacturer's instructions. Apply the slurry to the exposed concrete surface with an old paintbrush. To prepare the mortar, mix sand and cement in an old bucket or other container, in proportions of 1½ to 2 parts concreting sand to 1 part cement. Slowly add water and bonding agent, and mix well to produce a stiff paste.

3 **Applying the mortar.** While the slurry is still tacky, hold a timber batten against the front edge of the sill and use a bricklayer's trowel to fill in the exposed concrete with the mortar. Press the mortar down firmly and tamp it with the edge of the trowel to fill all cracks and crevices. Remove the batten. Smooth the surface of the mortar with the trowel or a steel float, then cover the sill with a polythene sheet and leave the mortar to harden for three days.

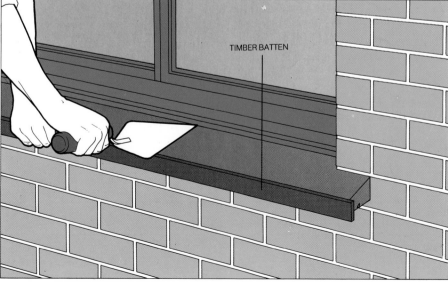

TIMBER BATTEN

The Anatomy of Blinds

A Venetian blind is a delicate affair, prone to frayed cords, torn tapes and bent or broken slats. Some repairs *(chart, right)* call for minor adjustments to the existing mechanism, but broken parts must be replaced by new ones from hardware shops, for which you will usually have to dismantle the blind. In the case of a frayed lift cord, however, you can thread a new cord through the slats and pulleys without having to take the blind down *(opposite page)*.

The most common problems with a simple roller blind—excessive or inadequate tension in the spring that rolls the blind up—are easily solved. To reduce the tension, raise the blind all the way and pull the flat end pin out of its bracket; then unroll the blind about half way by hand and replace the pin in the bracket. To increase the tension, pull the blind half way down, take the flat pin from its bracket and roll the blind up by hand. Repeat these procedures until the tension is satisfactory.

Diagnosing Venetian-Blind Troubles

Symptoms	Causes	Remedies
Bottom slats not horizontal	Lift cord misaligned	Raise or lower one side of lift cord until slats are level; set new alignment with equalizer catch.
Slats do not tilt	Tilt cord not aligned in pulley	Re-thread cord
	Tapes or braids disengaged from tilt rod	Secure tapes or braids to tilt tubes or rod with clips or staples
	Worm gear sticks	Lubricate gear with light oil.
	Worm wheel teeth disengaged from worm gear	Turn wheel by hand until teeth catch in gear.
	Worm wheel or tilt rod is out of guides	Reposition wheel or rod
Lift cord does not lock	Incorrect operation of blind	Pull and release cord diagonally on one side, then the other to find position of lock
	Cord out of lift-cord lock	Re-thread cord
Lift-cord lock catches too often or blind cannot be lowered	Incorrect operation of blind	Pull cord straight down and guide it straight up

The works of a Venetian blind. Two cords regulate the tilt and height of the slats in this Venetian blind. The tilt cord, on the left side, is linked *(inset)*—by a pulley, a worm gear and a tilt rod—to tapes at the front and back of the slats; pulling the cord raises and lowers the tapes to change the tilt of the slats. The lift cord, on the right side, passes over pulleys in the head rail and is knotted under the bottom slat or bar; pulling the cord straight down raises the bottom slat, stacking the others above it. An equalizer catch holds the ends of the lift cord in alignment to keep the bottom slat horizontal. The level of the bottom slat is fixed by a toothed lift-cord lock; when the cord is pulled diagonally, the teeth clamp it in place.

Other designs of Venetian blind have ladder braids in place of tapes and a metal rod in place of the tilt cord. On some models, a single ball-chain on a pulley both tilts the slats and raises and lowers the blind.

To dismantle a Venetian blind, remove the clamps that fasten the tapes or braids to the bottom slat or bar. Untie the knots at the ends of the lift cord and pull this cord free from the slats and pulleys. Pull out the slats horizontally and detach the tapes or braids from the tilt rod. For reassembly, reverse the procedure.

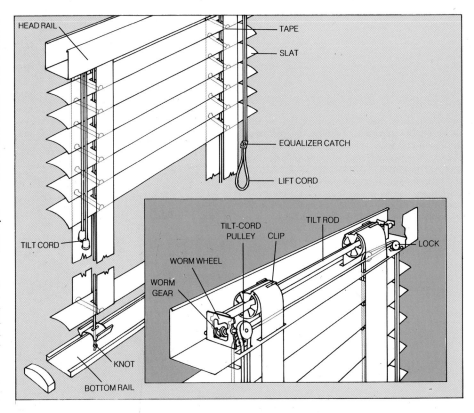

Replacing a Lift Cord
in a Venetian Blind

1 Attaching the new cord to the old. Cut through the loop of the old lift cord and slip the loose ends out of the equalizer catch. To calculate the length of the new cord to be fitted, multiply the full height of the blind by four. Attach the ends of the new lift cord to the cut ends of the old cord with adhesive tape or, if both cords are nylon, by melting the ends to be joined in a match or lighter flame *(right)* and then pressing them together with moistened fingers. The joints must be thin enough to pass through the holes in the slats, and they must also be strong; if a joint breaks while the new cord is being pulled through, you will have to take down the head rail and thread the new cord over the pulleys.

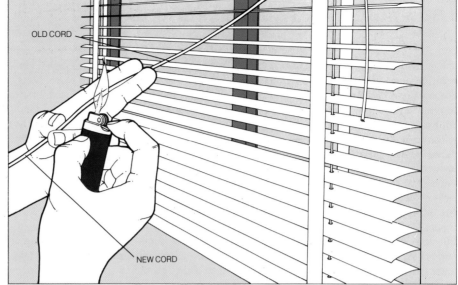

2 Pulling the new cord through. Let the blind fall to its full depth. Wedge the toothed lift-cord lock in the head rail with a piece of folded cardboard so that it will not clamp the cord. Remove the cap from one end of the lowest slat and slide off the bottom rail. Take hold of the knotted ends of the old lift cord at both sides of the blind and gently pull the old cord with the new cord attached through the slats and head rail.

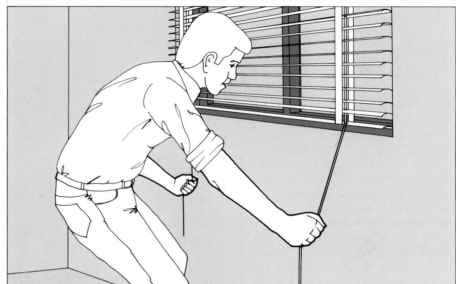

3 Securing the new cord. As soon as the joints between the old and new cords pass through the holes in the bottom slat, cut through the joints and tie a knot in each end of the new cord. Discard the old cord. Remove the wedge from the lift-cord lock. Pull the looped end of the new lift cord taut, check that the blind is hanging evenly, then slide the looped end through the equalizer catch. Replace the bottom rail and cap.

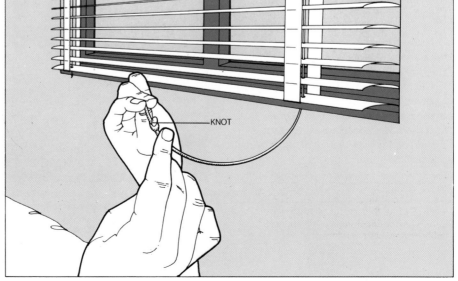

The Glazier's Craft: Cutting and Setting Glass

One day, by the law of averages, at least one of your windows will be shattered by a mis-hit ball or other projectile. Often, such an occasion provides an ideal opportunity to replace the broken pane of glass with a double-glazed sealed unit *(page 74)*. If the window is glazed with matching single panes of glass, however, you can simply cut and install a new pane of the same type.

The one essential tool you require is a carbide or diamond-tipped glass cutter. A pair of wide-nose glass pliers may be used to snap off waste glass after cutting, but the notches on the shaft of a glass cutter will serve equally well. To install a pane in a wooden frame, you will need raw linseed

oil putty to bed the glass in the rebate, and wedge-shaped metal fasteners called glazing sprigs to hold the pane in place. Metal-framed windows can be reglazed in the same way as wooden ones, but use metal casement putty (oil-based putty will not adhere to metal), and special glazing clips that slot into holes in the rebate.

To determine the size of a replacement pane, measure the inside of the frame after you have removed the remains of the old pane and all old putty, then subtract 3 mm from each dimension to allow for expansion. If the frame is badly out of square or an irregular shape, make a template pattern of the frame on a sheet of cardboard or

stiff paper. Get a professional glass merchant to make any cut longer than 1 metre: beyond that length, glass is difficult to handle, and a slip of the cutter will be costly. Large panes of glass must be supported by spacer blocks, which are set along the rebate as for a double-glazed sealed unit *(page 74, Step 1)*.

Before you cut a window pane, it is a good idea to practise on scrap glass first, to get a feel for the amount of pressure needed to score the glass for a clean cut. Too much pressure will crack the glass, too little will only scratch it. A rasping sound as you draw the cutter across the glass indicates that the pressure is right.

Safety Tips for Working with Glass

Cutting and handling glass are not dangerous so long as you take the following sensible precautions:

☐ Wear heavy leather work gloves for protection when handling loose panes or fragments of glass.

☐ Wrap broken glass in newspaper before placing it in a dustbin.

☐ Work with a helper whenever you carry panes larger than 1 square metre.

☐ Transport glass in several layers of newspaper on a padded surface (an old rug will do). Secure the pane by wedging a pillow at each side.

☐ Get a glass merchant to deliver any pane you cannot lay flat in your car.

☐ Before storing panes, mark them with a grease pencil or masking tape so they are easily seen.

☐ Cut glass on a padded surface.

☐ Immediately after cutting glass, brush fragments off the work surface.

☐ If the window is in a hard-to-reach location, remove the sash and work on a flat surface.

Clearing the Frame

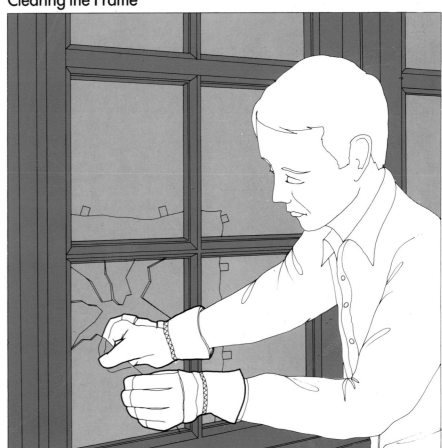

1 Removing broken glass. Tape newspaper to the inside of the window frame to catch glass fragments; then, from outside the house, work the shards of glass back and forth to free them. For an upstairs window, place newspaper on the floor and work from inside.

2 **Removing putty.** Scrape off the old putty with a hacking knife. To remove hard putty that adheres firmly to the rebate, tap the blade of the hacking knife with a hammer.

If the glass was held in place with lengths of beading, prise the beading off the frame with an old screwdriver or chisel.

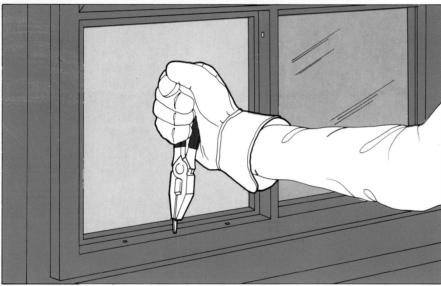

3 **Smoothing the channel.** Pull the glazing sprigs out of the frame with long-nose pliers and remove loose fragments of glass and putty with a wire brush. Sand the channel smooth and prime all exposed timber with wood primer.

Cutting a Rectangular Pane

1 **Scoring the glass.** Lay the glass on a padded surface, such as a scrap of carpet or a sheet of thin foam rubber. Brush linseed oil on the area to be scored and set a straightedge along the cutting line. Slanting the cutter towards you and holding it between your first and second fingers, pull it along the straightedge to score the glass in one smooth motion. Caution: do not go back over the score line—a double score will cause the glass to break with an uneven edge.

2 **Deepening the score line.** While a helper tilts one edge of the pane up from the work surface, tap the glass lightly along the underside of the score line with the ball at the end of the glass cutter; the blows will deepen the score. Then proceed to Step 3 immediately.

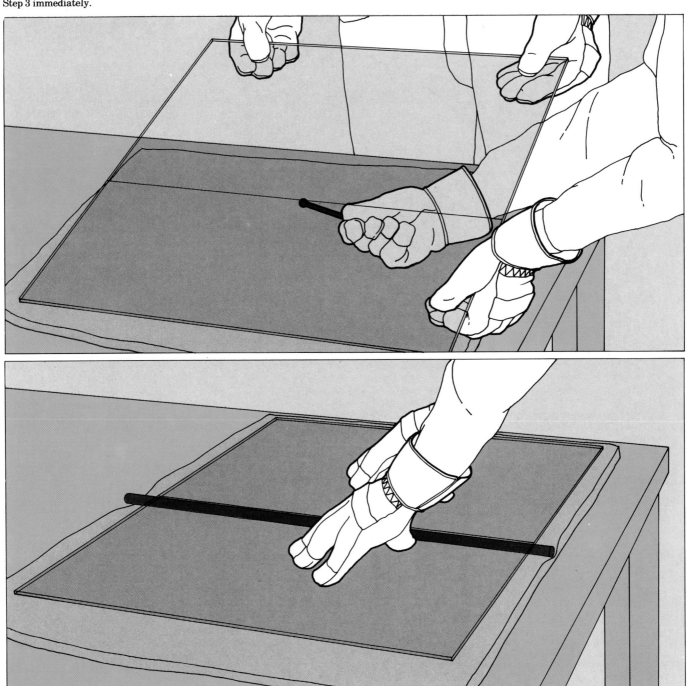

3 **Snapping the glass.** Place a thin rod such as a dowel—at least as long as the score line—on the work surface. Position the score line directly over the rod and press down firmly on both sides of the score; the pane of glass should snap cleanly. Use silicon carbide paper or an emery stone to smooth the new edge.

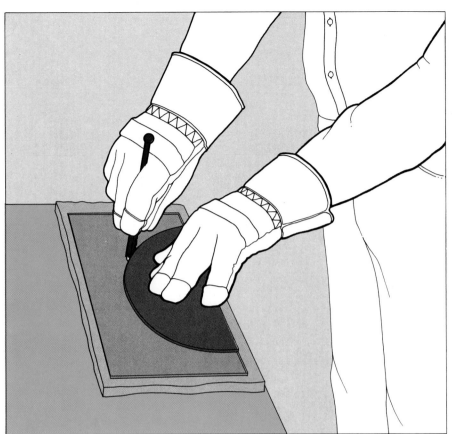

A Template for a Curved Cut

1 **Making the score.** Cut a hardboard template to the desired shape of the pane and set it on the glass; for the most common type of curved pane, which has one straight edge, align the template's straight side with the edge of the glass. Hold the template firmly, and make the score in a single motion from one end of the curve to the other.

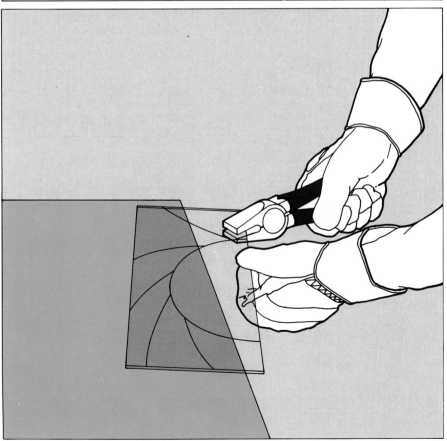

2 **Snapping the curve.** Scribe several radiating scores from the curve to the edge of the glass and tap under all the score lines *(opposite page, Step 2)*; then hold one edge of the glass over the end of the worktable and snap off the scored segments with a pair of glass pliers. Smooth the edge with silicon carbide paper or emery stone.

Setting Glass
in a Wooden Sash

1 Lining the frame. Soften a handful of linseed oil putty by kneading it in your hands; if the putty is very hard, add a little linseed oil. With the putty held in one hand, press a continuous strip into one of the rebates with your thumb. Continue until all the rebates are filled.

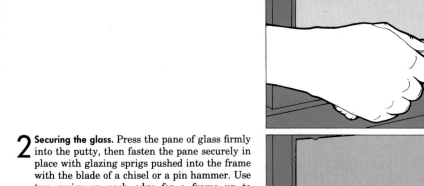

2 Securing the glass. Press the pane of glass firmly into the putty, then fasten the pane securely in place with glazing sprigs pushed into the frame with the blade of a chisel or a pin hammer. Use two sprigs on each edge for a frame up to 300 mm square, one every 100 mm for a larger frame. The sprigs must be inserted with their flat sides against the glass.

3 Bevelling the putty. Press additional strips of putty round the frame, then smooth the strips with a putty knife into a neat bevel that runs from the face of a sash or a glazing bar (sash divider) on to the glass. Shape the putty to form neat mitres at the corners. As you work, dip the knife in water from time to time to prevent it sticking to the putty. Scrape off excess putty with the knife. When the putty has hardened, paint it with undercoat and gloss paint to match the frame, extending the coat of paint 3 mm on to the glass for a weathertight seal.

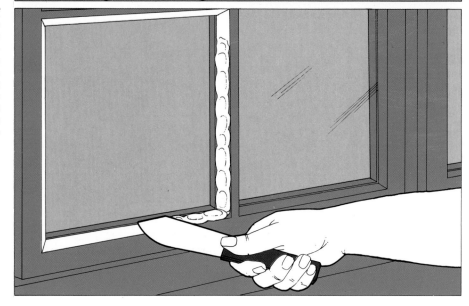

Tricks for Replacing a Glass Block

Glass blocks were fairly widely used from the 1930s to the 1950s and are now regaining a measure of their former popularity. Their return to fashion may have been stimulated by a growing concern over energy costs (a hollow glass block is a far better insulator than sheet glass), but other virtues of the material also played a part. Glass blocks allow the transmission of almost as much light as a pane of glass, while usually diffusing it for privacy.

Glass blocks are strong enough to guard against vandalism and burglary, but cannot support the weight of a structure above, so they must always be topped with a lintel. With this precaution, glass blocks covering an area of up to 2.5 square metres can be installed by a competent handyman. The mortar mix should consist of 1 part white Portland cement to 3 parts clean, fine, dry sharp sand, and the water should be mixed with equal parts of a liquid additive such as a styrene butodiene, to reduce shrinkage and help adhesion.

Larger areas should be installed by professionals; special hardware must tie the blocks to the surrounding structure, compensate for the different expansion rates of glass and other materials, and brace the blocks against wind.

Replacing a broken block requires no special hardware or skills, but the professional tricks on the right make for a faster, neater job. Finding a replacement block is quite easy: blocks come in a range of sizes and patterns, and any glass or builder's merchant should be able to help you match the new block with your existing ones. When mortaring in the block (*Step 2*), get a helper to hold a timber board against the block on the opposite side of the wall to prevent the mortar falling out.

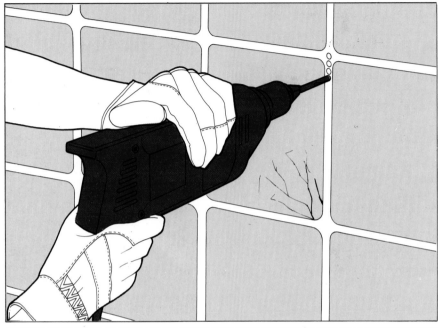

1 Removing the broken block. Using an electric drill fitted with a small diameter masonry bit, drill a series of holes in the mortar joint round the damaged block. To avoid disturbing any of the reinforcing rods that are embedded in the mortar joints, angle the drill slightly towards the broken block. Wear protective goggles and gloves while doing this. The holes should be as close together as possible without touching. Then carefully remove the mortar round the block with a chisel. When the mortar has been chiselled away, push the block through the wall. With a wire brush scrape off any mortar remaining in the cavity.

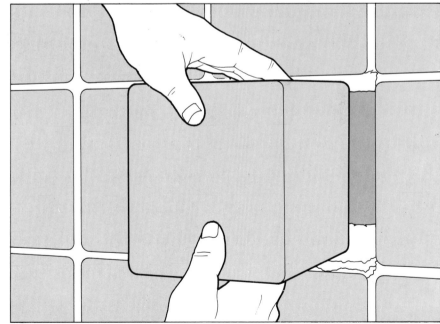

2 Mortaring in the new block. Lay a 12 to 13 mm bed of mortar on the bottom of the cavity, and gently slide in the new block. Push a long thin batten into the gap above the new block and tamp it down gently with a rubber mallet until the new block is aligned with the other blocks. Using a pointing trowel, push mortar into the top of each side joint and let it fall down the sides of the block, then tamp the mortar down with a piece of wood. Repeat this process, adding a little mortar at a time, until the side joints are filled, then trowel mortar into the gap above the block. Shape the new joints to match the existing ones, using a jointing tool or thin rod. Clean off any excess mortar immediately with a wet cloth.

Weatherstripping to Seal the Gaps

Gaps between doors or window sashes and their frames account for much of the heat lost from an uninsulated house. Sealing these gaps with an appropriate form of weatherstripping keeps warmth in and cold out, and has the added benefit of eliminating the noise of doors or windows banging against their rebates as they are closed.

A vast range of weatherstripping devices is now available, many of them designed for specific surfaces or areas. When choosing, remember that durability and finished appearance are often more important than cost or ease of installation.

Strips to seal gaps between a door or window sash and its surrounding frame are made in various materials and designs *(below)*. Self-adhesive strips and tongued strips that slot into grooves are usually secured to the face of the rebate or stop against which the sash or door closes; strips for nailing must be secured to the side face of the rebate or stop. For sash windows, plastic or spring metal strips are secured in the channels on each side of the frame and along the bottom rail of the top sash.

A versatile form of weatherstripping also used to seal cracks between the frame and the surrounding wall is silicone sealant; it is supplied in cartridges for use with a caulking gun *(opposite, below)*.

To seal the gaps under doors, the simplest draught-excluders are brush strips or lengths of flexible rubber or plastic secured in housings which are screwed to the bottom of the door. Also available are flexible threshold strips which are fixed to the floor between the two sides of the lining. Rather more sophisticated devices include spring-operated seals that are forced downwards as the door is closed; depending on its design, the casing for this type of excluder may be secured in a groove along the bottom of the door, so that the seal is concealed from view *(page 42)*.

The outside face of external doors should be protected by a wooden, plastic or aluminium weather bar in order to deflect rainwater from the bottom of the door *(page 43)*. Weather bars are available with co-ordinating draught-excluders and threshold strips; there is usually a groove or lip along the bottom of the bar to prevent water from seeping back under the door.

Before installing any form of weatherstripping, check that the window sash or door is not sagging or sticking, and make necessary repairs or adjustments. Surfaces should be clean, dry and in good condition; for silicone sealant, they may also need to be primed—read the manufacturer's instructions. All types of stripping must be carefully positioned—too tight a fit will impede the smooth opening and closing of the door or window; too loose a fit will render them ineffective.

Types of weatherstripping. Self-adhesive foam rubber strips or plastic V-strips are suitable for temporary installation only; they are inexpensive and simple to install, but can work loose easily. More durable types of weatherstripping for fixing with panel pins include a rubber strip slotted into an aluminium carrier, and a foam rubber strip sheathed in thin plastic and slotted into a PVC carrier. Brush pile strips, which often incorporate a flexible plastic strip down the centre of the pile for additional strength, are suitable for fixing to the moving parts of a window such as the rails and stiles of sliding sashes; the model shown has a ridged tongue that is slotted into a groove along the frame edge.

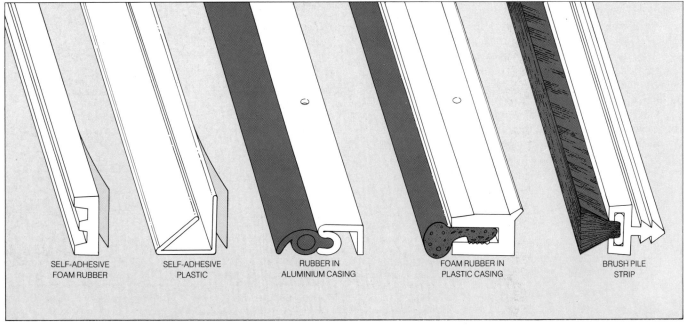

SELF-ADHESIVE
FOAM RUBBER

SELF-ADHESIVE
PLASTIC

RUBBER IN
ALUMINIUM CASING

FOAM RUBBER IN
PLASTIC CASING

BRUSH PILE
STRIP

Attaching Strip Seals

Self-adhesive stripping. Press the adhesive side of the stripping firmly against the rebate of the door or window frame, peeling off the protective backing as you work. On the hinge side, apply the stripping to either the side face of the rebate *(below)* or the closing face; along the top, bottom and opposite side, apply the stripping to the closing faces. At corners, cut the stripping with scissors or a trimming knife and butt adjoining lengths firmly together.

Stripping nailed to a door frame. Using a junior hacksaw, cut a length of stripping to fit down the inside of one jamb. With the door closed, hold the stripping in position with its flexible edge pressed gently against the face of the door, then secure the stripping with panel pins driven through the punched holes. Cut two more lengths of stripping; one to fit down the opposite jamb and one to fit across the frame or lining head, and attach these in the same way.

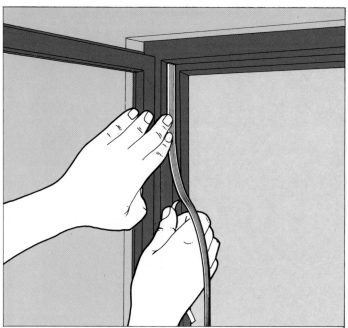

Applying Silicone Sealant

Using a caulking gun. Prime surfaces to be sealed as specified in the manufacturer's instructions. Insert the sealant cartridge in a caulking gun and cut the nozzle to give a bead slightly wider than the gap to be filled. Holding the caulking gun at an angle of 45 degrees to the surface, gently squeeze the trigger and draw the gun along the rebate to apply a continuous bead of sealant. At the end of each stroke, release the trigger and pull the gun away from the frame.

To prevent freshly applied sealant from sticking to the door or window sash, apply a releasing agent such as petroleum jelly or washing-up liquid to the relevant surfaces. Close the door or sash, leave the sealant to dry for the time specified by the manufacturer, then open the door or sash and remove the releasing agent.

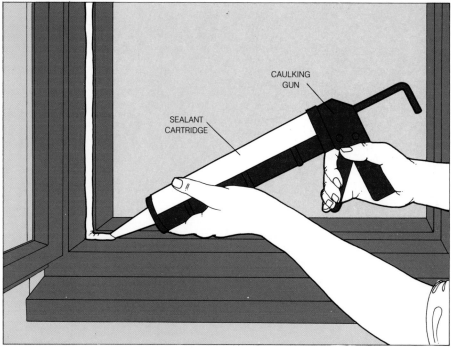

CAULKING GUN

SEALANT CARTRIDGE

Fitting a Concealed Draught Excluder

1 **Cutting the groove.** Remove the door from its lining and secure it in a vice or door jack *(page 103)*. Check the manufacturer's instructions concerning the depth and width of the groove to be cut *(inset)*. Using a mortise or marking gauge set to the groove width and centred between the sides of the door, score lines along the bottom edge of the door. Set the depth stop on a router to the groove depth, adjust the side fence as necessary, then switch on the router and begin to cut along one of the scored lines. At each end of the groove, move the router bit into the door edge from outside the groove in order to prevent the wood from splintering. Complete the groove by routing along the second scored line.

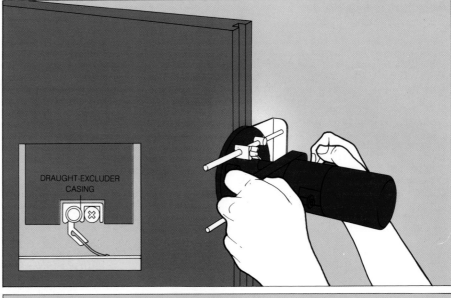

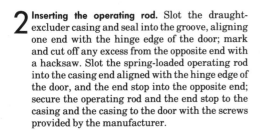

DRAUGHT-EXCLUDER CASING

2 **Inserting the operating rod.** Slot the draught-excluder casing and seal into the groove, aligning one end with the hinge edge of the door; mark and cut off any excess from the opposite end with a hacksaw. Slot the spring-loaded operating rod into the casing end aligned with the hinge edge of the door, and the end stop into the opposite end; secure the operating rod and the end stop to the casing and the casing to the door with the screws provided by the manufacturer.

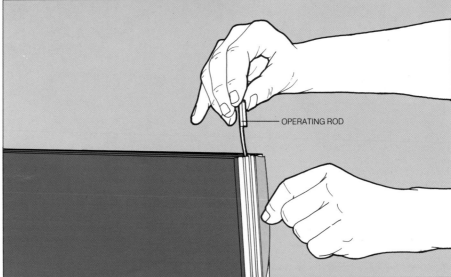

OPERATING ROD

3 **Fixing the striking screw.** Hang the door on its lining by reattaching the hinge leaves. At the bottom of the hinge side of the lining, mark the point of contact between the operating rod and the lining with a bradawl, and screw in the striking screw *(right)* or plate provided. As the door is closed and the projection on the operating rod is pressed inwards, the draught-excluder seal will be forced to the ground.

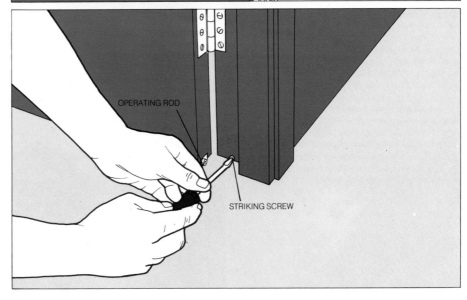

OPERATING ROD

STRIKING SCREW

Weather Bars
for External Doors

A wooden weather bar. Cut the weather bar to the exposed width of the door when closed; if the bar has pre-drilled screwholes, cut off equal amounts from both ends so that the screws will be spaced regularly. Plane the end of the weather bar that will be fitted to the lock side of the door at a slight angle, so that it will not catch against the frame rebate when the door is opened and closed. Position the bar flush with, or about 2 mm above, the bottom of the door, and attach it with countersunk brass, galvanized or sherardized screws, to avoid rusting. For additional protection, use a caulking gun to fill the narrow gap between the top of the weather bar and the door face with mastic sealant.

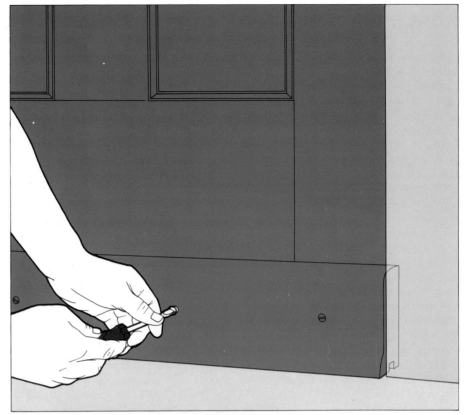

An aluminium threshold and weather bar. Using a hacksaw, cut both weather bar and threshold strip to the correct size. Lay the threshold strip in position and mark through the pre-drilled screwholes on to the step. Drill pilot holes and, if the step is concrete, insert plugs. Apply mastic sealant in the grooves on either side of the threshold strip, then screw the strip to the step with the screws provided. Hold the weather bar against the face of the door, then close the door and adjust the position of the bar until its groove is aligned with the projecting tongue of the threshold strip. Mark the screwholes on to the door, then apply mastic sealant in the weather bar grooves and attach the bar to the door with the screws provided.

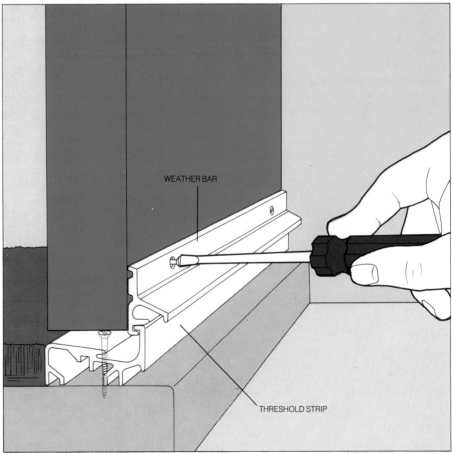

WEATHER BAR

THRESHOLD STRIP

Keeping Up Appearances: Decorating Doors and Windows

The paintwork or other finish applied to doors and windows is important not just for aesthetic reasons, but because it seals the timber or metal and provides protection against damp, rot and corrosion. The external surfaces of window frames are particularly vulnerable to the damaging effects of weather, and therefore require regular maintainance if they are not to deteriorate beyond repair.

Before attending to the window frames themselves, chip out any crumbling putty round the glass panes with a hacking knife or an old wood chisel. Brush out dust and debris from the rebates, prime or repaint any bare patches, then apply fresh putty—using linseed oil putty for timber frames and metal casement putty for metal ones. Defective caulking and pointing between the frame and the adjacent brickwork or masonry must also be chipped out and renewed at this stage.

Metal window frames are normally constructed of either aluminium or galvanized steel. Aluminium frames are usually left unpainted. On steel frames, remove small patches of rust with medium-grade steel wool and large patches with a scraper and wire brush; apply an appropriate rust preventer and then coat with metal primer. Scrape off any flaking paint with a stripping knife; sound paint should be abraded with wet and dry paper soaked in water, then rinsed and allowed to dry. Repaint both primed and abraded surfaces with one coat of undercoat and two coats of gloss.

On timber frames, remove flaking and blistered paint from flat areas with a stripping knife and from the mouldings with a shave hook *(opposite page, above)*. Paint that cannot be scraped off easily must be removed with a chemical stripper, a hot-air stripper or a blowlamp *(opposite page, centre)*. When using a chemical stripper, follow the manufacturer's instructions regarding the method of application and the length of time necessary for penetration, then use a stripping knife to scrape off the paint. Hot-air strippers and blowlamps should not be used on areas adjacent to glass because the heat can crack the panes.

Rub down with abrasive paper all areas from which paint has been stripped, then seal any knots in the timber with two coats of shellac knotting. Seal all exposed timber with a wood primer. Fill cracks in the timber or between joints with an appropriate wood filler *(opposite page, below)*, then prime again where necessary. Prepare areas of sound paintwork for repainting by rubbing down with wet and dry paper soaked in water; rinse the paintwork clean and allow it to dry before proceeding.

When you are painting window sashes and frames, apply both undercoat and top coat in the sequence described on page 46. Before applying the top coat, rub down the undercoat with wet and dry paper (600 grade) to remove any dust that has settled while the paint is drying.

For stripping and painting timber doors, follow the same basic procedures as for timber window frames. Wedge the door firmly open to leave both hands free for working, and place a dustsheet—or, if you are using a chemical stripper or a blowlamp, a piece of hardboard—under the door in order to protect the floor covering. Follow the painting sequence described on page 46, loading the brush lightly to avoid running drips. On a new door, remember to paint the top and bottom edges: the paint will not only seal the wood but also, on an exterior door, prevent moisture absorption.

Alternative finishes for timber doors and windows include a wide range of stains and varnishes, usually chosen to show off the natural wood grain. Ordinary dyes and stains are applied to bare wood and then coated with varnish; interior varnishes produce a hard surface designed to resist knocks and scratches, while oil-based exterior varnishes produce a surface that adjusts to dimensional changes caused by the weather. Careful preparation is essential because a clear finish will accentuate any scratch or surface blemish *(page 47)*. Old paint or varnish must be removed with a chemical stripper—a blowlamp can easily scorch the surface of the timber.

Conventional varnishes applied to exterior surfaces generally have a short lifespan because ultra-violet rays from the sun can penetrate the surface and destroy the adhesion between timber and varnish. Moisture is then absorbed by the timber, leading eventually to the growth of mould and rot. For external doors, one suitable finish is a woodstain that contains a fungicide and a pigment that protects the timber against ultra-violet light. Woodstains are available in a wide range of colours which can be mixed, and on new wood they are applied over a base coat of light or dark preservative *(page 47)*.

When applying any new finish, always check the manufacturer's instructions regarding suitability, method of application and the number of coats necessary. Work on a warm, dry day if possible, and ensure good ventilation; if you are working indoors, keep windows and doors open during both application and drying.

Preparing Surfaces for Paint

Using a stripping knife. Scrape off flaking paint from flat areas with a 75 mm stripping knife. On timber surfaces, use only the minimum pressure needed to remove the paint, and work along the direction of the grain where possible to avoid tearing wood fibres. Along mouldings and in difficult corners, use a triangular or combination shave hook *(inset)*. After using a stripping knife to remove paint that has been treated with a chemical stripper, clean the stripped surfaces according to the manufacturer's instructions, to neutralize any stripper remaining on the timber.

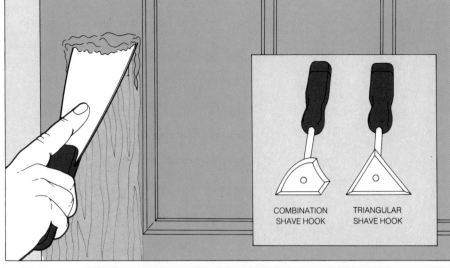

COMBINATION SHAVE HOOK   TRIANGULAR SHAVE HOOK

Using a blowlamp. Move curtains and other inflammable materials away from the working area, and protect floor coverings against burning paint with a sheet of hardboard. Hold the blowlamp about 75 mm from the paint and keep it moving backwards and forwards to avoid scorching the surface. As soon as the paint begins to soften and blister, scrape it off with a stripping knife, working in the direction of the wood grain where possible. If you are right-handed, hold the blowlamp in your left hand and the stripping knife in your right; on horizontal surfaces work from right to left, on vertical surfaces from the bottom upwards. Keep the blowlamp away from window panes or glass panels in doors because heat can cause the glass to crack. Scorched surfaces must be sanded right back to the bare wood before they are painted.

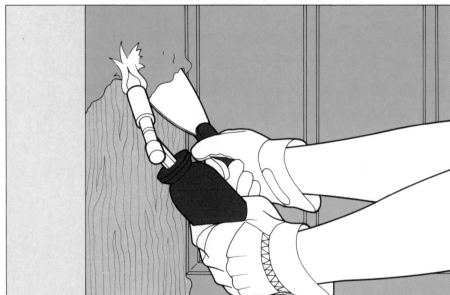

Filling cracks. Rake out dust and debris with a scraper, then slightly enlarge the crack and undercut the edges with the scraper to provide a firm base for the filler. Use a filling knife to press plastic wood filler or a similar appropriate filler into the crack *(right)*. When the filler has dried, sand the surface flush with the surrounding timber and prime it. For deep or large cracks, build up the filler in layers, allowing each layer to dry before applying the next.

Guidelines for Painting

Doors. Remove handles, hooks and other surface furniture, and wedge the door firmly open. On all doors the hinge edge should be painted the same colour as the side that closes against the stop or rebate, and the closing edge should be painted to match the other side.

On a flush door *(far left)*, paint the edges first, then use a 60 or 75 mm brush to paint a wide band at the top, covering about a quarter of the door. Apply the paint first by brushing in all directions, then brush vertically and finally lay off with horizontal strokes. Finish the door by working downwards in three further sections.

On a panel door *(left)*, paint the panels first, then paint the horizontal rails and any adjacent mouldings, and finally paint the vertical stiles and muntins together with any mouldings. Use a 50 mm-wide brush for the flat areas and a 25 mm brush for the mouldings.

Painting windows. For a casement window, open the hinged sashes wide and secure them. Taking care not to splash paint on to the glass *(opposite page, above)*, use an angled sash brush to paint the glazing bars first, then use a 50 or 25 mm-wide brush to paint the rails, stiles and edges of each sash. Brush strokes should follow the direction of the wood grain. Finally, paint the outer frame and, where appropriate, the sill.

On a sash window, begin by raising the inside sash and lowering the outside sash so you can paint the meeting edges, then follow the same sequence on each sash as for a casement window.

Neat edges for window panes. Round the inner mouldings on windows paint should overlap on to the glass panes by about 3 mm, to provide a watertight seal between the glass and the glazing compound. To make neat edges and to prevent paint from splashing on to the glass, stick masking tape on the panes *(right)* or hold a metal or plastic guard against the glass as you paint the mouldings *(far right)*. Masking tape must be removed immediately after painting, because paint that has been allowed to dry would be torn from the glass when the masking tape is peeled off. Use an angled sash brush—the pointed tip is especially useful for painting internal corners—and take care not to overload the brush.

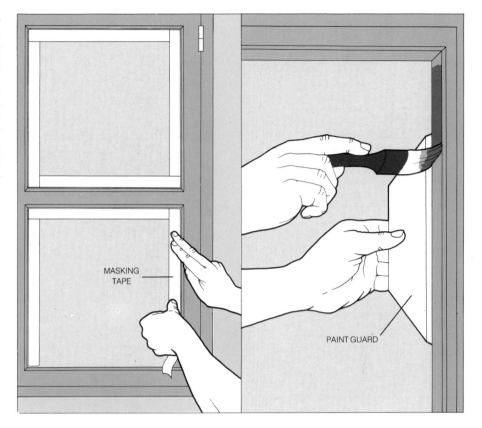

MASKING TAPE

PAINT GUARD

Applying Stains and Varnishes

Preparing the surface. Strip off old paint or varnish with a chemical stripper, then sand down the surface with fine-grade paper wrapped round a sanding block. Always work in the direction of the grain, using firm, moderate pressure. At the joints between rails and stiles, where the grain runs in different directions, use a cardboard shield to prevent the sanding block cutting across the grain of an adjacent section *(right)*. After sanding, brush off dust and debris with a fine brush, again working in the direction of the grain. Fill cracks with a stopper.

Stains and varnishes must be applied strictly according to the manufacturer's instructions. On new timber, a base coat of preservative may be necessary. Follow the sequences recommended for painting doors and windows *(opposite and above)*, and finish with brush strokes along the grain. To avoid unsightly patches, take care to apply an even coat: avoid overlaps, and do not let the edge of one section dry before you cover the adjacent section. End grain along door or window edges must be coated liberally. Clean brushes and wipe off splashes with white spirit.

2 Openings for Doors and Windows

Accessories for an opening. An L-shaped steel lintel will support the non-loadbearing veneer of brickwork above a window opening on the outside of a timber-frame wall. The concrete sill, which will finish the bottom of the opening, will be cast on site *(pages 58–59)*; once in place it will overhang the edge of the wall and deflect rainwater off its sloping surface. To knock out the opening, a lump hammer and a bolster will be used.

A new door or window begins with a hole in a wall or even the roof—and for some home owners that fact alone justifies calling in a professional. Cutting or breaking a large hole in either the protective skin of a house or an interior wall seems an awesome undertaking until you know exactly how to do it. In a timber-frame partition wall, making an opening is a simple matter of removing vertical supports called studs. To make an opening in a roof for a roof window, the rafters can be cut in much the same way. But in a masonry wall you must break out rows of bricks or concrete blocks using a bolster, a chisel and a lump hammer. And in a timber-frame house with a brick veneer, you make the opening by using a combination of both methods: first you break through the brick veneer outside the house, then you move indoors to remove the relevant studs of the inner leaf. To discover how the wall you plan to break through is constructed, read pages 50–51 carefully.

Such a hole does not threaten the structure of the house so long as you take adequate precautions. Bracing is needed when the wall you breech is a load-bearing wall *(pages 50–51)* which supports part of the weight of the house, and also when you cut through more than one roof rafter *(pages 68–69)*. A load-bearing wall requires temporary bracing until a strong lateral beam—called a lintel—can be installed as a permanent support. In a masonry house, a variety of types of lintel can be used *(page 57)*. In a timber-frame house with a brick veneer, both a wooden beam, called a header, for the inner leaf of the wall, and a steel lintel for the outer leaf, are required. Like load-bearing walls, rafters also need supporting while an opening is cut through the roof for a new window; once the opening has been made, timbers called trimmers are fitted as permanent bracing, which also completes a rough frame ready to accept the new window.

In some cases you need permission for this kind of work. The local building department will review plans for the opening (they should be drawn to scale) to make sure that the work complies with the building regulations. An official inspection of the job may be required, and in some localities inspections are made at several stages.

Make sure you have everything you need, including the door or window you plan to put in, timber and adjustable props for temporary supports. Order the lintels ahead of time or, if you plan to cast one on site *(page 57)*, gather the necessary materials. And for any type of exterior opening, get a sheet of heavy-duty polythene to shield the exposed opening from the wind or rain. Store materials in a garage if you can; otherwise, use the room in which you will make the opening—because the work is dirty, you will have to clear this room of furniture in any case. Recruit helpers in advance to measure the opening and to move heavy lintels and lengths of timber. And remember that after the job is done, you will be left with a small mountain of debris and may need to hire a skip to dispose of it.

The Anatomy of Interior and Exterior Walls

To add a new door or window to a house you must first cut an opening in a wall. This task is well within the capability of a competent amateur, but the technique will depend on the type of wall to be breached. Before you start, make sure you understand the wall's structure and functions, so you can restore it to full use afterwards.

The six main types of wall shown below and opposite reflect changing fashions in building techniques, and are grouped into two categories: solid walls (below) and cavity walls (opposite page). Houses built before about 1920 almost always have solid walls of brick or stone. Stone walls, which sometimes have a rubble infill, are easily penetrated by damp; in more modern houses both exterior and interior walls of solid construction are likely to be built of brick or blocks. Exterior solid walls incorporate a damp-proof course (DPC) just above ground level, to block upward move-

ment of ground moisture, and are often rendered with mortar on the outside.

Cavity walls, which comprise two parallel "leaves" separated by an air gap of at least 50 mm and connected by metal wall ties, have been increasingly used for exterior walls since about 1920. The air gap provides thermal insulation and prevents water from penetrating to the inside of the wall. From the 1950s, lightweight concrete blocks with improved insulating qualities have been used instead of brick for the inner leaf. Equally common in new houses today are timber-frame exterior walls, which usually consist of a load-bearing inner leaf of timber studs sheathed with boards and insulation material, and a non-loadbearing outer leaf of brick.

Inside walls, if they are not solid brick or block, are usually stud partitions. In older houses, the timber studs are covered with lath and plaster. Modern stud partition

walls consist of a framework of vertical timber or metal studs covered with plasterboard; for non-loadbearing walls "dry partitioning"—prefabricated panels joined by a cellular plastic filling—is often used.

If you plan to cut an opening more than 1 metre wide in a load-bearing wall, the weight borne by the wall must be temporarily supported with props and boards before any of the structure is removed. To provide permanent support after the job is finished, you will also need to install a lintel across the top of the opening. It is therefore vital to determine whether or not a wall is load-bearing before you begin work.

Exterior walls are almost always load-bearing, for the weight of the roof and upper floors runs through them to the foundations. Interior walls may or may not be load-bearing, and you will often have to carry out detailed exploratory work to discover which they are. First, sound out the

Six Types of Wall Construction

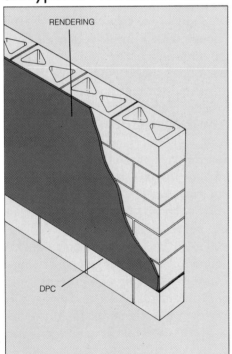

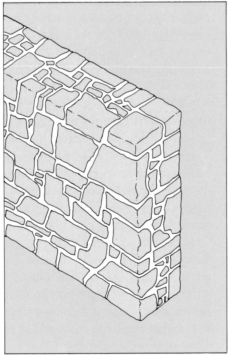

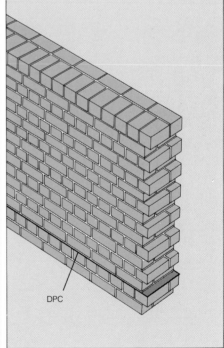

Solid block. In exterior walls (above), concrete blocks are built over a DPC just above ground level, and are rendered on the outside. The cavities within the blocks provide thermal insulation. Interior walls built with breeze blocks or lightweight concrete blocks are faced with plaster or plasterboard on both sides.

Solid stone and rubble. This traditional type of exterior wall has regular outer faces and a random rubble filling, and is usually much thicker than solid block or brick walls. Strength is ensured by "bonders"—wide stones that stretch three-quarters of the way across the wall. Internal stone walls are usually built to the width of a single stone.

Solid brick. In a double-thickness exterior wall (above), bricks are laid in interlocking patterns to avoid joints falling one above the other; the pattern shown here, English bond, is made up of alternating courses laid lengthwise and widthwise. Interior walls may be single thickness and faced with plaster or plasterboard.

wall by tapping it with a hammer. If the wall sounds solid, check whether it is load-bearing by lifting the floorboards of the room above to expose the joists: non-loadbearing walls usually run parallel to the overhead joists, while those that carry weight run at right angles to them. This test alone, however, may not be sufficient; some interior walls run through the floor overhead to bear the weight of the floor above or the roof. And the lower sections of such high internal walls, even if they do not carry a floor or the roof, still bear the weight of their own upper sections.

An internal wall that sounds hollow when tapped is a stud partition—there will be dead spots corresponding to studs. The wall is probably non-loadbearing, but in older houses stud partitions sometimes support joists and it is advisable to continue your examination as for a solid wall.

If the sound given out by a wall when it is tapped is not sufficiently clear for you to determine whether it is solid or not, cut a test hole through the plaster or wallboard within the area of the planned opening. If you have any doubt as to whether a wall is load-bearing or not, seek the advice of a professional architect, builder or surveyor. Professional advice must also be sought if there are visible cracks in the wall structure or if, after breaking through the wall covering, you discover cracks, or areas of damp or crumbling mortar between the bricks or blocks—these signs may indicate that the wall in unsafe, and you must not proceed before a full inspection and possible remedial work has been carried out.

Because all structural alterations in a house are subject to building regulations, you must check with your local building control officer before starting any work. Openings in internal walls do not usually require official permission, but the installation of a new window or external door close to an adjoining property, or in a house that is in a conservation area, will almost certainly require planning consent.

Finally, after finding out the legal requirements with which your work must conform, and determining the structure of the wall and whether it is load-bearing or not, there is a further factor to be taken into account. A wall on which electric power sockets are located carries live cables within it, and in older houses the presence of a nearby gas outlet may indicate that it also carries pipes. Either of these may restrict the size or position of your planned opening, or it may even need to be rerouted. In the case of electric sockets, turn off the electricity supply at the mains, then carefully chip away plaster round the socket to determine the direction of the cables—if these run across the area you plan to knock out, they must be rerouted by a professional electrician. In the case of gas pipes, seek the help of your local Gas Board.

The procedures for knocking an opening in brick or block walls, both solid and cavity, are outlined on pages 54–57; those for breaching an exterior brick veneer timber-frame wall are on pages 61–65; and those for making a door opening in an internal stud partition, on pages 52–53.

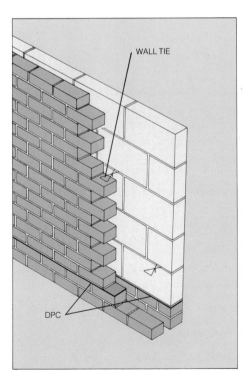

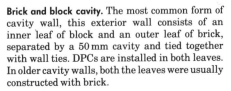

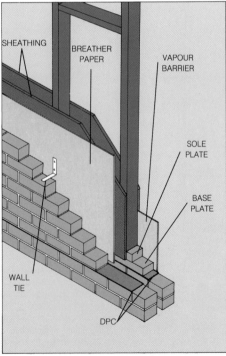

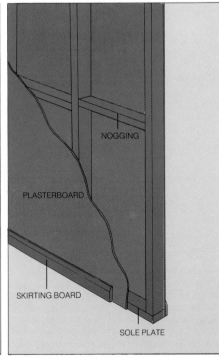

Brick and block cavity. The most common form of cavity wall, this exterior wall consists of an inner leaf of block and an outer leaf of brick, separated by a 50 mm cavity and tied together with wall ties. DPCs are installed in both leaves. In older cavity walls, both the leaves were usually constructed with brick.

Timber frame with brick veneer. The load-bearing inner leaf of this exterior wall consists of a framework of vertical studs, crosspieces and sheathing boards built over a DPC and solid base. A vapour barrier and breather paper are attached to the sheathing boards. The outer veneer of brick is not load-bearing.

Stud partition. This interior wall consists of a framework of vertical timber studs fixed to head and sole plates and faced with plasterboard. Horizontal noggings between the studs reinforce the framework. In older houses the studs may be covered with lath and plaster.

Framing a Doorway in a Timber-Stud Partition

To make an opening for a door in a stud wall, one or more of the timber studs must be removed to be replaced by a framework that will support the plasterboard covering and the door. The framework—a rough doorframe—must be built to the dimensions of the new door and its lining, so it is best to buy the door and lining before you start work, to ensure you build the rough frame to the right size *(pages 94–95)*.

If the wall is load-bearing *(pages 50–51)* you must provide temporary support for the structure while you cut the opening; use the same techniques as for a load-bearing timber stud exterior wall *(pages 62–63)*. Decide on the doorway location and draw a rough outline of the opening.

Within the outline, make a test hole in the plasterboard and locate the studs. If the doorway position is not crucial, you can position the opening to butt one edge against an existing stud. This stud can then be used as one side of the rough frame. Usually, however, you will have to cut the plasterboard back to the nearest studs beyond each side of the outline, and install new studs to create the sides of the frame. Each of these must be strengthened with additional reinforcing studs nailed to the inside of the opening *(Step 2, below)*.

The top of the rough frame is formed by a short crosspiece called a header, fixed between the studs. In a non-loadbearing wall, the header can be a single piece of timber; for a load-bearing wall, a more substantial beam is required *(pages 63–64)*. Short cripple studs, inserted between the header and the head plate of the wall, pro-

vide a surface for nailing fresh plasterboard at the top of the completed opening, and additional fixing for the header.

Since the plasterboard will have been removed by cutting along the edge of the existing wall studs, you will also have to provide nailing surfaces for the new plasterboard at the sides of the opening. Nail pieces of 100 by 25 mm timber inside the studs, flush with the stud surface.

To finish joints between new and old plasterboard you will need jointing compound, in powder form or pre-mixed. Pre-mixed compound is easier to work with than powder, since the consistency is uniform. To apply the compound, you will need a jointing applicator or a filler knife, a taping knife for embedding tape and a sponge for smoothing each application.

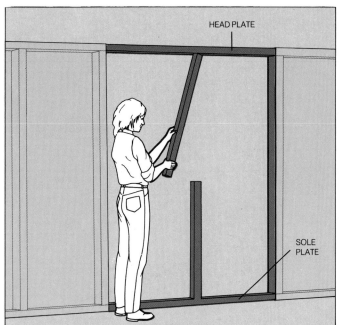

HEAD PLATE

SOLE PLATE

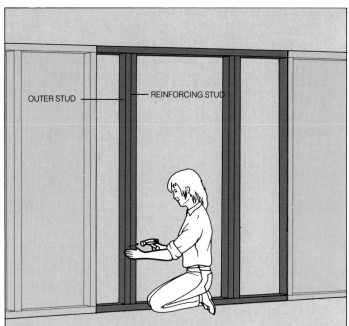

OUTER STUD — REINFORCING STUD

1 **Removing the plasterboard and studs.** Turn off all electrical circuits leading to the section of the wall to be cut out and remove the skirting board. Outline the opening on the wall, then cut the plasterboard back to the nearest studs beyond your marks using a saw. If you use a power saw, wear a face mask. Saw the intervening stud or studs in half near the middle, and work the halves free from the nailings, leaving the head and sole plate in position *(above)*.

2 **Positioning the studs.** Cut two outer and two reinforcing studs from 100 by 50 mm timber, to fit between the head and sole plates. Mark the location of the doorway on the sole plate and, allowing enough room for the doorframe and lining, plus 6 mm clearance on either side, mark the position of the new double studs. First checking for plumb, toenail the outer studs to the head and sole plates. Use three 75 mm round-wire nails in each joint—two on one side and a third centred on the other. Position the reinforcing studs against the inside of each outer stud and toenail them into the head and sole plates, using two nails for each joint. Nail the double studs together every 400 mm with 100 mm round-wire nails.

3 **Installing the header and cripple studs.** Cut a 100 by 50 mm header to fit between the double studs. Mark the position of the header on the studs by measuring up from finish floor level the height of the doorframe and lining, plus 6 mm for fitting. Cut two cripple studs from the discarded wall studs, making them long enough to fit between the head plate of the wall and the top of the planned header. Nail the cripple studs to the full length studs, using 100 mm round-wire nails. Position the header between the full length studs; check for level and insert packing if necessary. Fix the header by nailing from beneath into the cripple studs *(right)* and toenailing into the full length studs. Cut away the section of sole plate between the reinforcing studs and make good the floor if necessary.

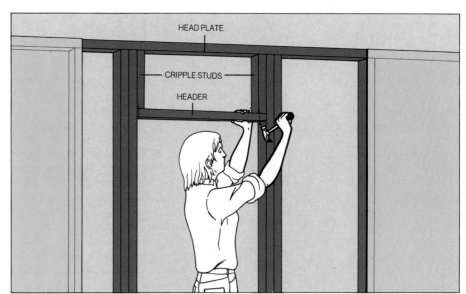

4 **Fixing new plasterboard.** Cut two additional studs to fit between the head and sole plates, and nail them to the studs at the sides of the original opening. Measure the distance between the plasterboard and the inside of the doorway on both sides of the opening, and cut two full length pieces of plasterboard to fit. Lift one into position; if it is heavy make a foot lever from two scraps of wood to aid lifting. Starting at the top, drive plasterboard nails into the underlying stud at intervals of about 200 mm. Set the nails about 9 mm in from the board edges. Cut a piece of plasterboard to fit above the doorway and nail it in place in the same way *(right)*. Hammer all the nail heads just below the plasterboard surface, ready for making good later.

5 **Finishing the joints.** Cut strips of jointing tape to the length of each joint plus about 50 mm, and place them in water to soak. Using a jointing applicator, spread jointing compound along the joints between the old and new plasterboard. Starting at the top of each joint, press one end of the soaked tape into the wet compound and embed the tape in the compound with a taping knife *(right)*. Smooth the joint to a feathered edge. Cover the nail dimples with compound, then apply two further coats of compound, allowing it to dry before each new application. When the final coat is dry, smooth the joints with fine glass paper on a sanding block, taking care not to damage the surface of the plasterboard.

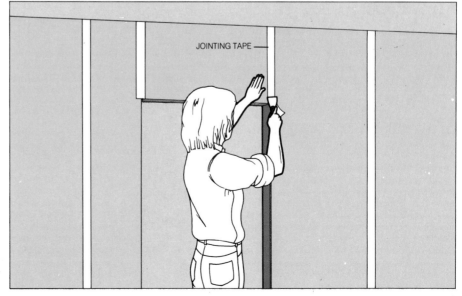

How to Break an Opening Through a Masonry Wall

Breaking through a load-bearing masonry wall, whether exterior or interior, demands careful planning and preparation. A large opening cut without proper precautions can distort windows and doorframes, push interior walls out of shape, and even weaken the house structure.

If a new door is to be installed, the rough opening should be about 10 mm wider than the width of the frame and lining and about 6 mm higher. For a window, allow the same clearances as for a door, unless you plan to rebate the reveals of the opening *(page 60)*. In this case cut the rough opening to the width of the frame minus twice the depth of the rebate. If possible plan the opening along mortar lines and, for a doorway that is sited in an exterior wall, align the bottom of the opening with the existing horizontal damp-proof course.

Small openings of 900 mm or less may not need propping—the bricks above the opening should support themselves. But before larger openings are made, weight borne by the wall must be redistributed through temporary supports—adjustable props, timber boards and transverse beams called needles—that transfer the load to the ground inside and outside the house. Floors which are supported by the wall must also be propped separately. Inside the house, props are required to take the load down to solid ground; the props, which support both the needles and floors, should form continuous lines between storeys.

Before cutting the opening you must install a lintel as permanent support for the wall. Ready-made lintels are available in a variety of materials, shapes and sizes, to suit different needs *(page 57, above)*. Alternatively, you can make a lintel on site *(page 57, below)*. Seek advice about the size of lintel you need or, if you are making one, about the size and number of the reinforcing rods required for your situation.

For a cavity wall, follow the same procedure as for a solid one, marking the opening first on the outside, then on the inside by drilling through to the inner leaf. As the lintel height is greater on the inside of the wall, mark its dimensions separately on each leaf before positioning the needles. When breaking out the opening, work first on the outer leaf, then on the inner one. At the sides of the opening, line the inside of the outer leaf with a vertical DPC and cut bricks to size to close the cavity.

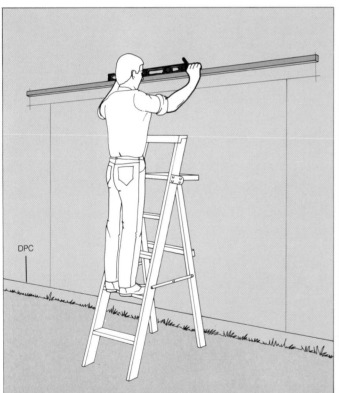

1 **Marking the lintel and opening position.** Using a straightedge and spirit level, outline the proposed opening on one side of the wall; for an exterior wall, as here, mark the outside. If the wall is rendered or plastered, chisel away a small piece just above one of the corners to determine the position of the nearest brick or block course. Ensuring that the top of the lintel will coincide with the bottom of a course below, draw in the dimensions of the lintel. Allow at least 150 mm overhang at either end to rest on the bearings.

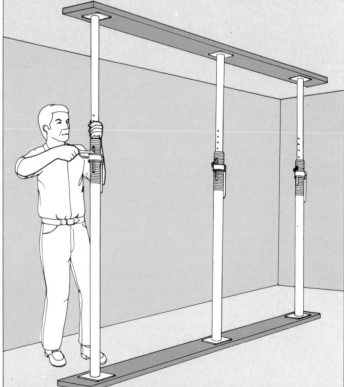

2 **Positioning the supports.** Working inside, place adjustable props on a timber board, up to 600 mm from the wall and no more than 900 mm apart. Set another timber board above the props to distribute the load. Continue propping upwards, between storeys, to the roof joists; if there is a basement or under-floor area, prop the floor beneath in the same way. Brace any window openings above the work area by placing vertical timbers into the reveals at either side, and wedging horizontal ones between them.

3 **Making the needle holes.** On the exterior wall, mark positions for the needles about 200 mm or two brick courses above the lintel and 150 mm in from either end. If the marks are more than 900 mm apart, you will need an intermediate needle. Drill through the wall to transfer the needle marks to the other side, then, using a cold chisel, bolster and lump hammer and working from both sides of the wall, cut square holes big enough to take the needles—they should be 75 or 100 mm square structural-grade timber and long enough to protrude 600 mm on either side of the wall. Clean all the mortar from the top of the holes so that the needles, when inserted, will bear directly on the masonry.

4 **Inserting the needles.** With a helper, slide the needles through the wall; they should protrude by equal amounts on both sides. Place a timber board on the ground, beneath the ends of the needles, on both sides of the wall. Prop each end and check that the props are vertical. Then, with your helper checking for level, tighten the props in turn until the needles are pressed firmly against the tops of the holes. Secure the props by nailing through the end plates into the timber boards and needles.

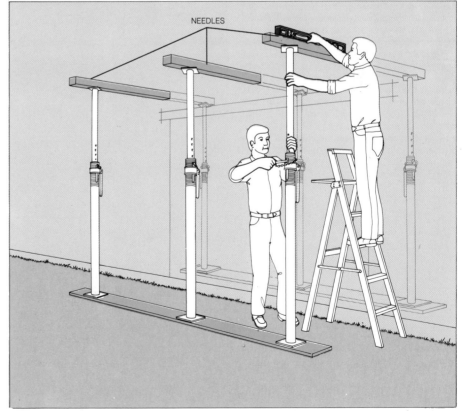

NEEDLES

5 **Cutting the channel for the lintel.** If the wall is rendered, use a lump hammer and bolster to chip away the rendering and expose the masonry within the area marked for the lintel, plus 25 mm all round. Carefully remove the bricks within the lintel area, course by course, working on both sides of the wall if necessary. Clean out all the mortar on the courses below and above the channel to ensure a level bearing, then install the lintel *(opposite, above)*. Always wear protective goggles while you work.

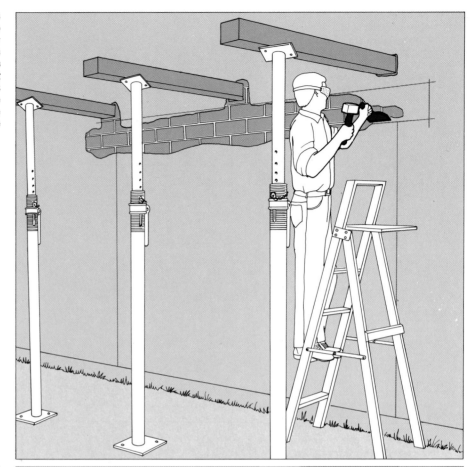

6 **Knocking out the opening.** Drill through the wall to transfer the markings for the opening to the other side. Remove all the interior plaster and exterior rendering within the outline of the opening. Using a lump hammer and bolster, or a heavy-duty electric hammer with a chisel attachment, carefully remove the first course of bricks beneath the lintel. Working from side to side, knock out the rest of the opening, a course at a time. Check the dimensions of the opening, then trim off any protruding brick-ends, and fill gaps with bricks cut to fit. Finally, chisel off all the plaster and rendering up to about 100 mm from the edge of the opening and round the needles, ready for making good later.

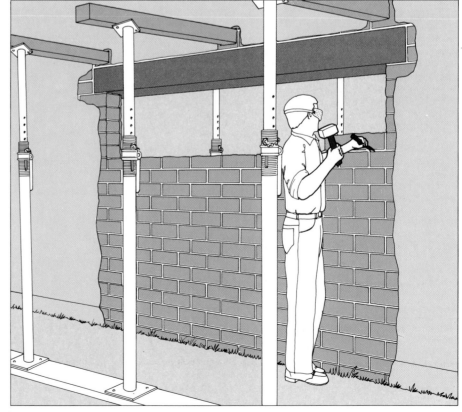

A Choice of Lintels

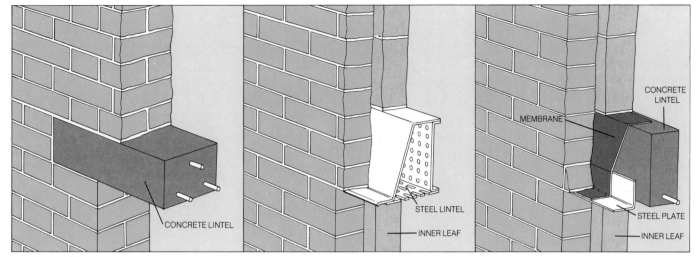

CONCRETE LINTEL

STEEL LINTEL

INNER LEAF

MEMBRANE

CONCRETE LINTEL

STEEL PLATE

INNER LEAF

Installing the lintel. The lintel must suit the wall structure in which it will rest. In the solid brick wall *(above, left)* a concrete lintel reinforced with steel rods is used to span the thickness of the wall. For a cavity wall, choose a boot-shaped lintel *(above, centre)* or a combination such as the concrete plank and L-shaped steel lintels *(above, right)*. The thick vertical section of the boot supports the inner load-bearing leaf and the outer leaf rests on its toe. When made of galvanized steel, the boot can be used with no DPC. With the combination lintel the concrete plank carries the load while the L-shaped steel piece supports

the outer leaf. A flexible damp-proof membrane should be inserted during installation.

To fit a lintel, cut a channel to the correct size *(opposite, Step 5)*. In a solid wall, lift the lintel into place, spread mortar in the gap and lever the lintel upwards with a crowbar. To wedge it in position, slide slates between the lintel and the bearings at each end. When installing a boot lintel in a cavity wall, remove one course of bricks in the outer leaf, and inside remove enough courses to accommodate the vertical section of the boot. Working inside, place the lintel in the opening and make good the walls. The technique for in-

stalling the combination lintel is similar: remove enough courses inside to make room for the thick concrete plank. Working inside, lay the damp-proof membrane over the lower edge of the opening, then slide in the L-shaped lintel so its base rests on the outer leaf, under the membrane. Pull the membrane up to cover the vertical side of the L-shaped lintel and, with someone still holding the membrane up, slide the plank lintel into place. Lay the free end of the membrane on top of the plank lintel. Mortar in the bricks on the outer leaf; make good inside, levering up the plank lintel as for a solid wall.

A Lintel Cast *in situ*

Making the lintel. Mark the opening and lintel position *(page 54, Step 1)* and prop if necessary. Knock out the masonry within the lintel outline. Remove a course of bricks or blocks the length of the lintel above the opening, and a course below, but only to the width of the finished opening.

To build a form for the lintel, cut a base from 25 mm exterior-grade plywood to fit the bottom of the opening and lay it in place. Pack slates or wedges under the base, until it is level with the end bearings. Cut two 25 mm-thick side pieces, to the same size as the lintel opening plus an allowance all round for fixing *(inset)*. Position one side piece with its top level with the top of the lintel position and nail it firmly to the wall and into the base. Secure the second side piece in the same way. Paint the inside of the form with a proprietary releasing agent, linseed oil or varnish. Place small blocks of wood crosswise along the base, and lay the reinforcing rods on them. To prevent the form from distorting under the weight of the concrete, nail 50 by 25 mm cleats across the top between the side pieces.

Make a wet mix of 6 parts ballast to 1 of cement. Use a trowel to fill the form with the concrete *(right)*, then tap the sides with a hammer to settle it. After two days remove the side pieces and make good above the lintel. After another day, remove the base and knock out the opening.

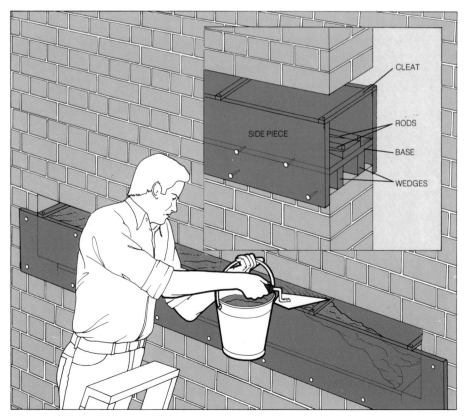

CLEAT

RODS

BASE

WEDGES

SIDE PIECE

Weatherproofing a Window Opening

To prevent the wall immediately beneath a window soaking up rainwater that will run down the glass panes, the bottom of a new opening must be protected by a sill *(right)*. If the sill that forms the bottom rail of the window to be installed is not wide enough to project at least 30 mm beyond the wall edge, you will have to bed a separate sill in the opening before fitting the window. Prefabricated sills are available in a range of standard sizes; alternatively, you can construct your own brick sill while finishing the opening *(page 65)* or cast a concrete sill in a mould *(right, below and opposite page)*. The procedure for bedding a concrete sill in the wall is shown on pages 78–79.

The most difficult part of casting a concrete sill is making the box mould *(Steps 1–2)*; it has to be strong enough to contain wet concrete, yet easy to dismantle once the concrete is dry, and its inside dimensions must correspond to the dimensions of the sill required. The length of the sill should equal the width of the wall opening plus approximately 120 mm to allow for the stooled ends that are bedded into the wall at each end; the depth should equal at least half the thickness of the wall (or, for a cavity wall, the thickness of the outer leaf and the cavity), plus 30 to 50 mm for the overhang; and the height of the stooling at the back of the sill must be at least 80 mm, allowing for a minimum height of 40 mm at the front of the finished sill. To guide you when cutting and assembling the components of the box mould, draw an end view and a plan view of the sill required, with all its dimensions marked.

A finished concrete sill. The sill extends the full width of the opening and about 60 mm into the wall at either side. The raised stooling at the back provides a flat seating for the window, and the stooled ends support the masonry or brickwork at the sides. The groove along the stooling may be fitted with a water bar to weatherproof the joint between the bottom of the window frame and the sill. The sloping surface of the sill carries rainwater away, and the drip groove underneath prevents water from running back along the underside of the sill by causing it to form large drops heavy enough to fall to the ground. On the inside of the wall, any part of the opening not covered by the sill is built up with bricks to the height of the sill after it has been installed.

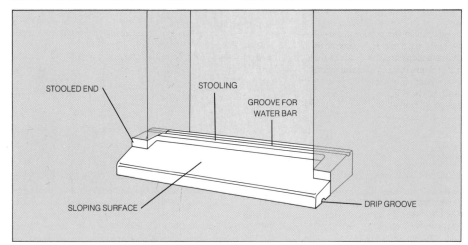

STOOLED END

STOOLING

GROOVE FOR WATER BAR

SLOPING SURFACE

DRIP GROOVE

Forming a Concrete Sill in a Mould

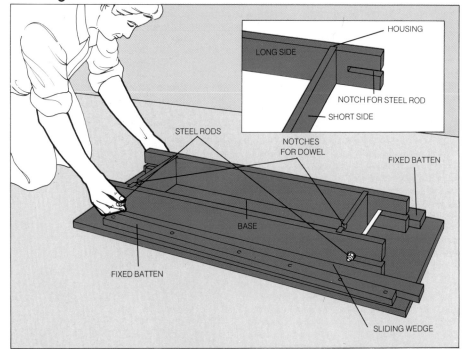

HOUSING

LONG SIDE

NOTCH FOR STEEL ROD

SHORT SIDE

STEEL RODS

NOTCHES FOR DOWEL

FIXED BATTEN

BASE

FIXED BATTEN

SLIDING WEDGE

1 **Making the box mould.** From 19 mm plywood cut to the maximum sill height required, cut the two short sides of the mould 16 mm longer than the depth of the planned sill, and the two long sides 80 mm longer than the sill length. At both ends of the long sides, cut 8 mm-deep housings for the short sides—the distance between the housings must equal the sill length—and cut notches to hold steel rods *(inset)*. Cut a notch 23 mm from one end of each short side to hold a length of dowelling. Cut a base approximately 60 mm longer and wider than the sides of the mould, and screw a batten along one long side. Slot the short sides into their housings and lay the box frame on the base, butting it against the fixed batten. Screw a second batten to the base on the opposite long side of the frame, at a slight angle. Cut a long wedge to slide between the second batten and the box frame to hold it securely. Fit steel rods, threaded at each end, into the notches in the long sides; secure them with nuts and washers.

2 **Completing the mould.** To make the splayed wedge that will form the sloping surface of the sill, cut a block of timber to the length of the sill; the depth of the block *(inset, distance A)* must equal the depth of the sill's sloping surface, and its height *(B)* must equal the height of the stooling less the height of the sill front edge. Mark off the dimensions of the stooled sill ends at both ends of the block and cut out the waste. Along the long side from which the waste was cut, mark off the height of the stooling above the sloping surface *(C)*, then plane or saw down to this line to create a sloping surface. Butt the splayed wedge against one long side of the box frame and nail it to the base. If a water bar is to be fitted when installing the sill, cut 19 by 6 mm dowelling to the length of the sill and nail it to the base 15 mm from the opposite side of the box frame.

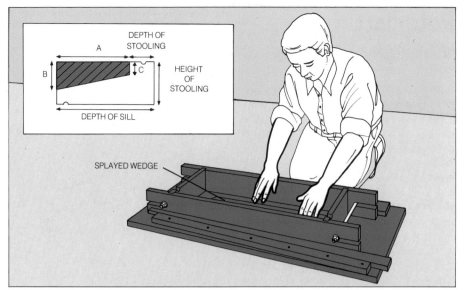

3 **Filling the mould.** Paint the inside of the mould with a proprietary releasing agent, clean oil or varnish. Make a wet concrete mix of 4 parts sand, 2 of ballast and 1 of cement. Pour in the concrete to about 25 mm below the top of the mould. Lay 6 mm steel reinforcing rods on top of the concrete, bedding them in firmly with the side of a trowel. Pour in more wet concrete to fill the mould to the top, then vibrate the mould by tapping its sides with a hammer to compact the concrete. Brush a length of timber dowelling with releasing agent and lay it between the notches in the short side pieces *(right)*. Scrape off the excess wet concrete by drawing a straightedge across the top of the mould.

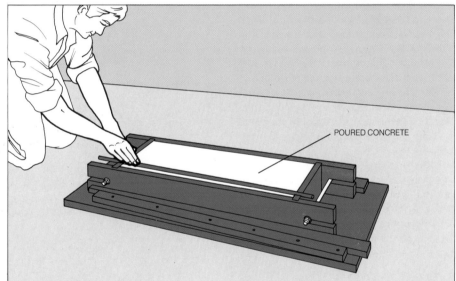

4 **Removing the mould.** Allow the concrete to set for at least two days, then remove the steel retaining rods and knock out the sliding wedge to release the sides of the box. Leave the sill for another day or two to dry out completely, then lift it from the base and fit it in the opening *(pages 78–79)*.

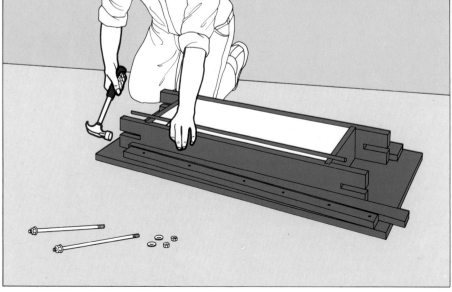

Rebating Window Reveals

Before installing a new window you may have to make a rebate in the opening. Although most modern frames do not require rebates they are often used as a means of weatherproofing. The exterior masonry will cover the sides of the frame and prevent water from penetrating the wall at the jambs. With traditional box frame windows—which are usually custom-built these days—the opening must be rebated.

The depth of the rebate *(right, above)* will be determined by the size and style of the frame. Modern frames with narrow jambs will need a rebate no more than 30 mm deep. Anything larger could spoil the appearance of the window and block the sashes. Box frames will require the width of the lining less about 25 mm on either side. The width of the rebate will vary according to the position of the frame in the wall. Often this is governed by the size of the sill and the type of wall construction. In a cavity wall, for example, the frame will usually be centred to bridge the gap between the two leaves.

Before making a rebate ensure that the end bearings for the lintel above the opening will still be at least 150 mm on either side—anything less could weaken the lintel. When cutting the rebate use battens, fixed to the reveals and the inner face of the wall, as guides.

1 Cutting the rebates. Determine the width of the rebates; mark this on the reveal at either side of the opening and draw a vertical line from top to bottom. Assess the depth of the rebates and mark the wall on either side of the opening this distance from the reveals. Draw lines from top to bottom of the opening at these marks, and check that they are the same distance apart as the width of the window frame. Cut four timber battens to the height of the opening and tack them along the lines outside the area marked for the rebates; use masonry nails driven part of the way into the mortar joints. Using the battens as a guide, cut into the masonry with a hammer and bolster, then chip out all the masonry within the marked area to form a clean, square rebate. Remove the battens. Repeat for the other side.

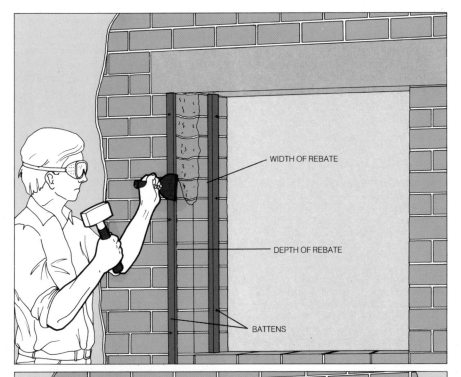

WIDTH OF REBATE

DEPTH OF REBATE

BATTENS

BATTENS

2 Rendering the reveals. If the wall is rendered on the outside you will need to render the reveals to match. Fix battens to either side of the new reveals, so that they project about 10 mm beyond the masonry. Wet the wall between the battens, then mix mortar from 5 parts of soft sand to 1 of cement. Using a steel or wooden float, apply the mortar to the dampened masonry. Allow the mortar to dry slightly, usually about 10 minutes, then working upwards from the bottom of the opening, draw a straight-edged piece of wood across the battens with a sawing action to smooth the surface of the mortar *(right)*. Leave the mortar to dry for a day, then remove the battens. Repeat for the other side. Make good the exterior wall before installing the new window.

Cutting an Opening in a Brick-Clad Timber-Stud Wall

Fashioning a door or window opening in a timber-frame house with brick cladding differs from making an opening in a solid masonry wall. Because the wall consists of two independent leaves *(pages 50–51)* you must make two openings—one from the outside and one from within—using different techniques for each.

The exterior opening is made first. The outer leaf, called a veneer, is a single thickness of brick which acts as a protective facing. As it is not load-bearing, it can be cut without the temporary propping techniques used to support solid masonry *(pages 54–55)*. Before you knock out the opening, however, you must install an L-shaped steel lintel as a permanent support for the brickwork above.

Start by marking the proposed outline on the wall and adjusting it, if necessary, to coincide with mortar lines *(page 54)*. Score only the horizontal mortar joints at the sides of the marked opening. When all of the whole bricks within the opening are removed, a series of notches, called a saw-tooth pattern, will remain. To fill the gaps in the saw-tooth pattern, you will have to cut some of the old bricks into odd-sized sections called bats. To make a bat, score a brick with a cold chisel. Then place the brick on a bed of sand and hammer the chisel sharply along the line; the brick will break cleanly along the scored line.

The inner load-bearing leaf must be temporarily braced with adjustable steel props *(page 54, Step 2)* while the studs are being cut. It is then permanently supported by a heavy timber framework built round the opening. The sheathing between the two leaves will also have to be cut precisely to the size of the opening.

After breaking through the inner leaf, install the framework: this consists of a header, which bridges the top of the opening, and short jack studs which carry the load from the ends of the header to the existing sole plate. To form the jambs of the opening, additional framing studs are toe-nailed to the sole plate and the header. Pieces of timber inserted beneath the head plate transmit weight down to the header. But if the top of the header falls within 50 mm of the head plate, you can eliminate these by making a wider header, and setting it against the head plate. Ask an architect or structural engineer to determine the header size you need.

If you are making a doorway, cut both openings down to the level of the finish floor. When installing a new window, you will need to build a rough frame in the inner leaf in order to support the window board; in the outer leaf you can install a sub-sill of concrete or brick, which will help deflect rainwater from the new window opening *(pages 58–59 and 65)*.

An Opening in Brick Veneer

1 **Scoring the opening.** Wearing goggles and a face mask, use an angle grinder fitted with a masonry disc to score the horizontal mortar joints in a saw-tooth pattern. Score joints to the first vertical joint outside each side of the marked opening. Score the bottom of the opening along a horizontal mortar joint. Score the top of the door opening along a horizontal joint and score a corresponding line two courses above for the top of the lintel channel. Caution: work slowly to avoid overheating the grinder.

2 **Starting the lintel channel.** At an upper corner of the scored opening, chip through horizontal and vertical mortar joints with a lump hammer and a cold chisel or bolster. From each of the two courses above the lintel opening, remove two or three bricks. Immediately below, from the top course of the opening, remove three more bricks *(above)*. Try not to break the bricks you remove: you will need some undamaged bricks to fill the space above the lintel.

3 **Attaching veneer supports.** Screw a 50 mm angle bracket into each stud behind the sheathing you have exposed. Use 50 mm No. 8 galvanized wood screws and place the upper flange of the angle bracket snugly against the brick above it. Cut out the remaining bricks from the three brick courses and attach a bracket to each stud.

4 **Completing the channel.** Remove the bottom course of bricks from the lintel channel, then chisel out an additional 200 mm of brick at each end of the course to make supporting surfaces, called bearings, for the lintel.

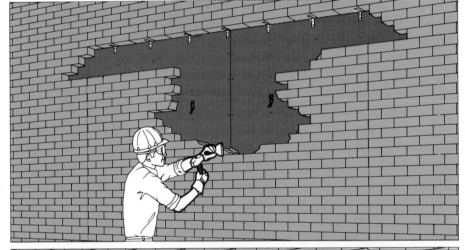

5 **Completing the opening.** Using a lump hammer and bolster, remove most of the bricks within the opening. As you near the edges of the opening, chisel out the remaining bricks one by one in the scored saw-tooth pattern.

Cut several bricks to fill the saw-tooth pattern at one side of the opening. Add 9 mm to the width of your door or window unit and brick in the other side to create an opening of this width.

6 **Setting the lintel.** Apply a 15 mm bed of mortar to the top of each end bearing; then, with the aid of a helper, lift the lintel into the lintel channel, with the horizontal flange on the shoulders and the vertical flange against the sheathing. Place a spirit level on the horizontal flange and tap the high end of the lintel into the mortar with a hammer until the lintel is level.

7 **Filling in the channel.** With a heavy-duty staple gun, fasten a length of 450 mm-wide plastic damp-proof course (DPC) to the sheathing between the lintel and the angle brackets. Lap the DPC completely over the lintel, then cut it with a pair of scissors, leaving 10 mm of the horizontal flange exposed. Spread a thin layer of mortar on the DPC which is over the horizontal flange, then lay a course of bricks directly on top, substituting a piece of 9 mm fibreboard 100 mm long for mortar in every third vertical joint between the bricks *(inset)*. When the mortar has set, pull out the pieces of fibreboard, leaving weep holes for escaping moisture. Brick in the remaining courses, varying the thickness of the mortar beds and joints to match those at the sides of the opening.

FIBREBOARD

Framing for a Door in a Load-Bearing Stud Wall

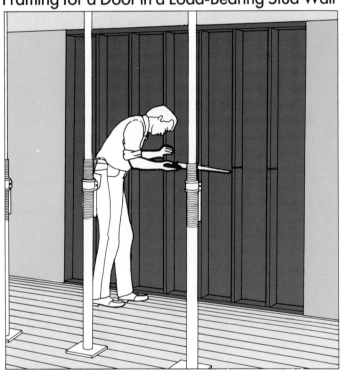

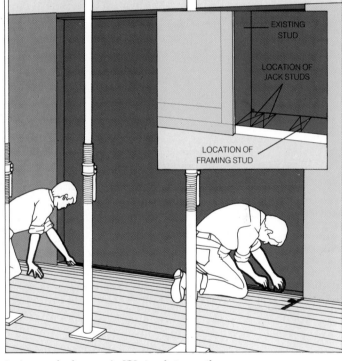

EXISTING STUD

LOCATION OF JACK STUDS

LOCATION OF FRAMING STUD

1 **Removing the studs.** Working from the outside, drill through the wall to mark the opening on the inner leaf. Then, working inside, take off the skirting board and remove the plasterboard covering the studs, cutting it back to the next stud at either side of the proposed opening *(pages 52–53)*. Remove the insulation and the vapour barrier from between the studs. Set adjustable props to take the weight of the ceiling above *(page 54, Step 2)*. Make two saw cuts about 25 mm apart through the middle of each stud within the planned opening. Knock out the 25 mm pieces and complete the cuts with a wood chisel. Prise the studs away from the sheathing with a crowbar. Cut off the nails that protrude from the head and sole plates with a hacksaw.

2 **Laying out the framework.** Measure between the outer edges of the side jambs of the finished door, add 25 mm (or the shimming space specified by the manufacturer) and draw lines this far apart on the sole plate, centred on the desired location of the finished unit. Mark positions on the sole plate for two framing studs, one at either side of the doorway, and two pairs of jack studs, one pair next to each of the existing studs at the sides of the opening *(inset)*.

3 **Putting in the jack studs.** Measure the height of the doorframe, add 10 mm (or the dimension specified for packing space by the manufacturer), and mark each of the existing studs at the sides of the opening at this total height above finished floor level *(right)*. Cut four 100 by 50 mm jack studs to the length between the mark on each existing stud and the sole plate. Nail the jack studs to the plate, the existing studs and each other, using 100 mm round-wire nails spaced at 300 mm intervals.

PLASTERBOARD

EXISTING STUD —

4 **Installing the header.** Make a header of the size required by the opening, by nailing together two lengths of 225 by 50 mm timber. With the aid of a helper, position the header so it rests on the jack studs *(right)*. Toenail up through the jack studs into the bottom of the header, and through the header into the existing studs. To fill the gap between the header and the head plate of the wall, cut pieces of 100 by 50 mm timber to fit, and toenail them at 400 mm centres to the head plate and the header.

Cut two framing studs that will fit between the header and the sole plate. Align the framing studs with the marks made on the sole plate *(page 63, Step 2)*, check that they are vertical, then toenail them in place. To complete the opening, saw through the sheathing, using the framing studs and header to guide the saw. Remove the sheathing. Then cut away the sole plate between the framing studs.

HEAD PLATE

HEADER

JACK STUDS —

Completing the Opening for a Window

Adding an interior rough sill. Cut through the studs just above the level of the bottom of the finished window opening *(page 63, Step 1)*, and remove only the top section of each stud. Install jack studs and a header following the techniques on pages 63–64, Steps 2–4. Measure down each pair of jack studs the height of the window frame plus 60 mm; use the marks as guides to snap a chalk line on the intervening studs, then cut the studs at the lines with a jigsaw. Nail an extra short stud to each inner jack stud between the sole plate and the mark for the rough sill. Cut a 100 by 50 mm rough sill to fit between the jack studs and nail it to the short studs *(right)*. Cut two framing studs to the distance between the rough sill and the header, mark off the width of the window on the rough sill, then align the framing studs with these marks and toenail them to the rough sill and the header. Finally, cut through the sheathing, using the header, rough sill and framing studs to guide the saw.

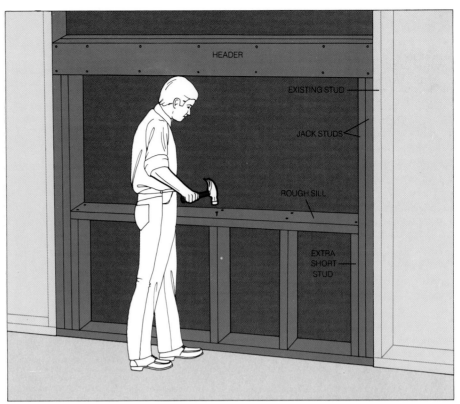

HEADER

EXISTING STUD

JACK STUDS

ROUGH SILL

EXTRA SHORT STUD

ROWLOCK COURSE

Making an exterior sill. Finish the bottom of the opening in the brick veneer to match the other windows in your house. If the other openings have a row of bricks laid on edge across the bottom, lay a matching row—called a rowlock course—across the new opening, leaving a 10 mm gap between the back of the brick course and the interior wall structure. Lay the back of the mortar bed about 10 mm thicker than the front, so that the bricks will slope to shed water *(above)*; adjust the thickness of the bed to bring the top of the bricks to the same level as the interior rough sill. Adjust the mortar joints between bricks so that you finish the course with a whole brick. Caution: the mortar must fill the joints completely in order to keep out moisture.

If ordinary courses—that is, whole bricks laid lengthwise, with their narrow edges showing—form the sills for the other window openings in your house, build the new sill in the same way, adjusting the thickness of the mortar joints between courses to bring the bricks flush with the level of the rough sill. You can buy a brick-faced concrete sill which is fitted as a unit. If the other openings have pre-cast concrete sills, order a matching pre-cast sill 120 mm wider than the new opening, or alternatively make one yourself *(pages 58–59)*. The procedure for installing a precast concrete sill is shown on pages 78–79.

Removing an Old Window or Door Lining

Often new windows and doors are installed in existing openings, to replace units that are faulty, rotten or simply old-fashioned. Before putting in the new frames or door sets, however, you will have to remove the old ones. The same techniques apply to both windows and doors.

The frame of a casement window is usually attached to the wall with nails or screws, or with lugs mortared into the brickwork or masonry. Once the window sashes have been removed, the exposed frame can usually be simply prised out of the wall; a neater and safer method, however, is to cut through the fixings (*opposite page, Step 3*), thus avoiding excessive damage to the wall.

Vertical sliding sash windows are often held only by wedges, which will come loose when the frame is knocked or levered out.

Because the restoration of external wall surfaces is more difficult than internal plastering, it is usually advisable—even for ground-floor windows—to work inside the house and lever the frame inwards.

1 Stripping the frame. To remove opening sashes from the window frame, unscrew the hinges from the jambs. On side-hung sashes, unscrew the bottom hinge of each sash first and work upwards, taking the full weight of the sash in your hands when the top hinge comes free. If the sash is attached with loose-pin butt hinges, simply pull out the pin to remove the sash. Remove glass from fixed lights by prising off the surrounding beading or by chipping away the putty and pulling out the glazing sprigs (*page 35, Steps 1–2*). Use a crowbar, and a wooden block to protect the wall surface, when prising off any architraves surrounding the frame (*page 23*). To remove nails from any architraves that you wish to re-use, grip the shanks of the nails firmly with pliers and pull them through the architraves from the back side.

2 Exposing the frame-to-wall joint. Using a club hammer and a cold chisel or bolster, chip away any internal plastering that covers the joint between the wall and the frame jambs, head and sill. It may also be necessary to chip away rendering on the outside of the wall— but work carefully to avoid damage to the brickwork or masonry.

3 **Cutting through the fixings.** At the top of one of the jambs, insert a hacksaw blade attached to a keyhole saw handle between the frame and the wall. Saw down the length of the jamb, cutting through the nails, screws or other fixings that secure the jamb to the wall, then repeat for the other sides of the frame. Most windows are secured with just two fixings in each jamb, but larger frames may have fixings in the head and sill also. On metal frames attached directly to the wall, unscrew the bolts securing the frame to lugs mortared into the wall *(inset)*; on metal frames attached to a timber subframe, undo the bolts in the metal frame and then cut through the subframe fixings with a hacksaw.

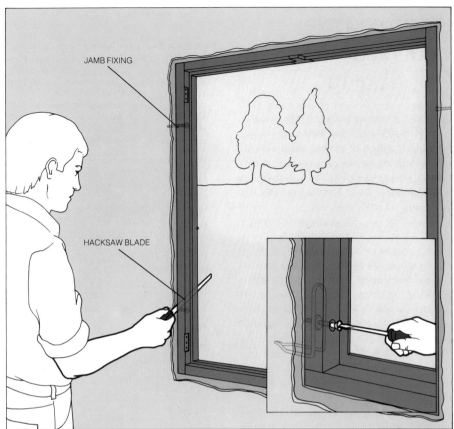

JAMB FIXING

HACKSAW BLADE

4 **Sawing through the jambs.** If the frame has now become completely detached from the wall, it may be knocked and levered out of the wall opening with a mallet and crowbar. If the frame is still stuck fast in the opening, saw through each jamb about 100 mm above the sill. The teeth of the saw will grate against mortar or masonry, so for this task use an old handsaw that is not needed for fine work.

5 **Removing the frame.** If the frame has integral mullions or transoms, saw through each member and knock out the cut sections with a mallet. Prise the jambs away from the wall with a crowbar *(right)*, then prise out the head and sill.

Cutting a Hole in the Roof

The installation of a window in a sloping roof can dramatically transform a dark and dusty attic into a potential new workspace or living area. But before any work commences, check with your local authority: the conversion of an unused attic into a habitable room demands careful planning and is subject to strict building regulations concerning ventilation, fire doors, headroom and the reinforcement of floors. However, the actual construction of a roof opening requires few tools and is a simpler task than breaching a masonry wall.

A small skylight can often be fitted into the space between two rafters, in which case the opening is made by simply cutting away the roofing felt, removing the tiles and sawing through the battens. But for a wider window, any rafters that run through the area of the planned opening must be securely supported with adjustable props before you saw through them. If—as will often happen—the width of the opening required does not coincide exactly with the space between rafters, you will have to frame one side of the opening with a false rafter after the top and bottom trimmers have been installed (*page 82*). If you need to relocate struts or purlins you must consult a professional, who will advise you how to redistribute the weight evenly.

The techniques shown here for supporting and cutting through the roof rafters apply to openings both for windows fitted flush with a sloping roof (*pages 82–83*), including skylights, and also for dormer windows (*pages 84–91*). All of the work can be carried out from inside the roof, but before starting have some plastic sheeting to hand in case of rain, and cordon off any adjacent throughways to protect passers-by from falling tiles.

1 **Marking the rafters.** Using a try square, mark the top of the planned opening across the underside of the rafter that will form one side of the opening. Align one end of a long straightedge with this mark, then nail it to the rafter. Using a long spirit level and the straightedge, transfer the mark to the rafter that will form the other side of the opening, and to any intervening rafter. If the planned opening does not fit neatly between rafters, mark the next rafter beyond the side of the opening. With a try square, extend the lines on the undersides of the rafters on to their side faces. Mark off the lower edge of the opening on the rafters in the same way.

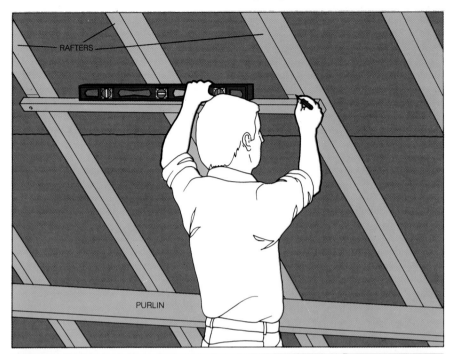

RAFTERS

PURLIN

ROOFING FELT

2 **Removing the felt and tiles.** Cut away the roofing felt within the area of the planned opening, leaving a 100 mm margin at the edges for making good when the work is finished. Then carefully remove the tiles within the marked area and ease them through the tiling battens one at a time; if necessary, break the first tile to be removed by tapping it sharply with a hammer. Take care not to let any of the tiles slip down the outside of the roof. To allow for the flashings, which are installed after the window frame has been fitted, remove tiles to one course above and below the marked area, and to one run on either side.

3 **Removing the battens.** Holding the saw flush against the inside face of the rafter that will frame one side of the opening, cut through the tiling battens. If the opposite side of the opening will also be framed by an existing rafter, repeat this procedure to cut away the battens at the other side. If the planned opening is narrower than the distance between the side rafters, mark the battens to the required width and saw them off; the cut ends of the battens must be supported by a false rafter *(page 82, Step 2)*.

4 **Supporting the rafters.** Get a helper to hold a 100 by 50 mm board above the opening and top pencil marks. Below each rafter to be cut, hold an adjustable prop perpendicular to the board. Rest the base on another 100 by 50 nailed to the floor joists, then fix a timber block behind the end plate to hold the prop in place *(inset)*. Tighten off the props and nail the top end plates to the board. If the bottom of the opening is more than 1 metre above a purlin, support the rafters below the bottom marks in the same way. Leave the props until trimmers are fixed *(page 82, Step 1)*.

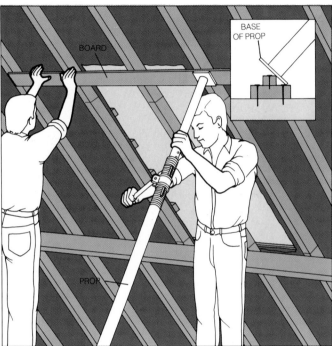

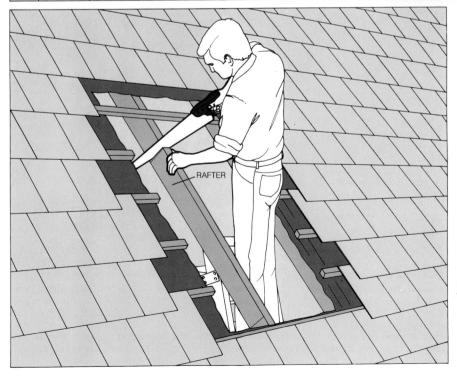

5 **Cutting the rafters.** Saw through any rafters running through the planned opening; hold the saw absolutely square to the rafter and cut carefully down the lines marked on the side faces. The opening is now ready to receive top and bottom trimmers and, depending on whether you plan to install a roof window *(pages 82–83)* or a dormer *(pages 84–91)*, either false or reinforcing rafters.

3 A Wealth of Windows

Ready for installation. A prefabricated timber frame rests in a window opening in a masonry wall. After the wooden shims round the sides have been adjusted until the window is correctly aligned, two holes will be drilled through each window jamb into the wall. The long screws with pre-fitted sleeves will then be driven home with the screwdriver, to secure the window.

According to master architect Le Corbusier, the history of architecture is largely the history of the window. In turn, the history of the window is largely the history of changes in technology and economics, changes which during the 20th century have been particularly rapid.

Innovations in architecture and in construction techniques in the early part of the century led to the development of pivoted and horizontal sliding windows, improvements in air and water-tightness, and the use of aluminium as a construction material for new windows. Many of these changes were first applied to commercial and public buildings only, but as industrial techniques for the production of both doors and windows were developed, they were adapted for residential property. By the 1950s the sliding sash window—a dominant feature of homes since the 18th century—had been largely superseded by the side-hinged casement window as the standard design for new houses.

Since the oil crisis in the early 1970s and the consequent rise in domestic heating costs, there has been a strong emphasis in window design on thermal insulation. A window is sealed only by glass, which is a poor insulator—1 square metre conducts as much heat as 10 square metres of wall. The use of double or even triple glazing can reduce heat conduction through glass by up to 50 per cent. Almost all new windows are designed to accommodate sealed units—layers of glass sealed together with an air space between—and kits for installing a second pane of glass over an existing one are widely available. Also, weatherstripping seals are now standard in most new windows, and both sashes and frames may have two or three rebates to improve airtightness.

Because aluminium, like glass, is a poor insulating material, it is now often combined with timber or plastic (uPVC), and windows made of uPVC alone are increasingly available. The machinery for making aluminium and uPVC windows is extremely expensive; such windows are made by large specialist firms, and must usually be fitted by the supplier or a professional installer. New or replacement timber windows may be supplied and installed by large companies in the same way, but they can also be bought or ordered from local builders' merchants or joinery firms and installed by the purchaser *(pages 78–81)*.

Another major influence on window design has been rising house prices, which have encouraged many owners to adapt or add on to their present homes rather than buy new property. Because of the high density of housing, particularly in urban areas, upwards rather than sideways expansion is more common, and roof windows specifically designed to light attic or loft conversions are now available *(page 82)*. Another popular option is the dormer window, which projects outwards from a sloping roof *(pages 84–91)*. These are not new: roof openings are as old as the builder's art, and dormers may go back a thousand years or more. According to legend, the dormer began in medieval Germany as a way to add rooms without adding taxes: German tax collectors assessed houses according to the number of their storeys up to the eaves.

Keeping Out the Cold: Double Glazing for Existing Windows

Although double glazing is not the most efficient method of insulation—draughtproofing, loft insulation and cavity-wall insulation all make a bigger difference to your heating bills—it does help to retain warmth, and also reduces outside noise and improves security. The least obtrusive and most effective double glazing for an existing window is a replacement, factory-made sealed unit, secured in the frame in place of a single pane of glass *(page 75)*; if your existing single-glazed windows are in good condition, however, a much cheaper alternative is secondary glazing.

Secondary glazing consists of a second pane of glass or clear plastic fitted to the frame or sash or into the reveal of an existing window. You may choose to construct your own wooden frame for secondary glazing to match the surrounding material, but a cheaper and quicker alternative is to buy

a kit containing plastic or aluminium sections together with their appropriate fixings. Sliding frames *(below)* fit into tracks that are usually secured in the window reveal; hinged frames *(page 74, below)* or fixed frames are usually fixed directly to the existing frame or sash. You may need to install a timber subframe inside the reveal for sliding frames if the sides of the reveal are not square, or if you wish to attach hinged or fixed secondary glazing over a metal frame. Hinged or sliding frames can easily be opened for cleaning or in an emergency, but fixed frames cannot be opened without removing the whole pane.

For efficient insulation, the gap between the existing and the new pane should be between 12 and 25 mm; for sound insulation a gap of at least 100 mm is recommended, but the design of the window often makes this impractical. To exclude

draughts and to prevent warm air leaking into the gap and causing condensation on the inside face of the outer pane, the seal round secondary glazing must be airtight.

Some secondary frames can be glazed with either glass or a plastic such as acrylic, polyester or polycarbonate. Plastics are usually lighter and tougher than glass, but they have several disadvantages: they scratch easily, are inflammable (and so can be damaged by a cigarette), carry a strong static charge that attracts dust, and their clarity gradually deteriorates with age. Ordinary float glass, 4 mm thick, is recommended for most secondary glazing; for windows vulnerable to damage, use toughened glass. Follow the frame manufacturer's instructions when measuring for a new pane; the glass may be cut by the supplier, or you can cut it yourself following the instructions on pages 36–37.

Fitting Aluminium Sliding Frames

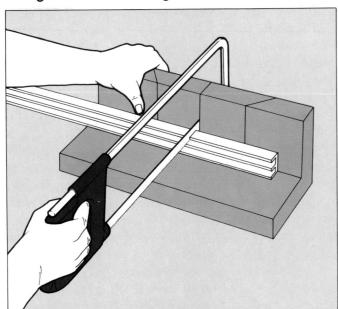

1 Cutting the tracks. Using a steel tape measure, measure the full width of the window reveal at the top and bottom. Mark these distances on two lengths of track and, using either a junior hacksaw or a fine-toothed hacksaw with a mitre box, cut the tracks at right angles. File the cut edges smooth. Cut to size lengths of the flexible draught seal supplied and slide them into the appropriate slots on the tracks.

2 Securing the tracks. Drill holes at intervals of about 300 mm in the base of the tracks, countersink the holes, then hold the tracks in position and mark the screwholes on to the top of the reveal and the sill. Drill pilot holes in the top of the reveal—using a percussion drill if drilling into a concrete lintel—then plug the holes and secure the track with 20 mm No. 8 screws. Secure the bottom track in the same way, but without using plugs if the sill is wooden. At each side of the reveal, measure the distance between the top and bottom tracks, cut lengths of track to fit and secure them with screws in the same way as for the top and bottom tracks.

3 **Cutting the glass.** Following the manufacturer's instructions, measure between the side tracks and between the top and bottom tracks to establish the dimensions of the glass panes. If the existing window has two or more panes separated by vertical stiles, calculate the horizontal dimensions of the sliding panes so that they will meet exactly in front of the stiles. Cut the glass to size or order it from a supplier.

4 **Fitting the framing sections.** For each glass pane, cut four aluminium framing sections and four lengths of rubber gasket slightly shorter than the sides of the pane—the exact measurements depend on the size of the corner pieces. Press a length of gasket on to one of the vertical sides of the pane, then press a framing section over it. Set a block of wood in the middle of the framing section and tap it sharply with a wooden mallet; then, moving the wooden block first to one side and then to the other, continue tapping with the mallet until the glass is firmly held by both gasket and framing section. Fit a gasket and framing section to the opposite side of the glass in the same way. Slide a handle on to the fitted section that will close against the side track, and secure it with the screw provided.

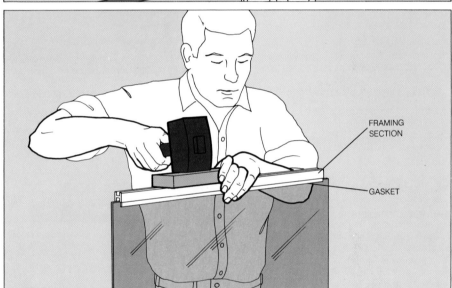

FRAMING SECTION

GASKET

5 **Fitting the corner pieces.** Press lengths of gasket on to the top and bottom edges of each glass pane, slide corner pieces into the ends of the top and bottom framing sections, and fit the framing sections over the gaskets by tapping with a mallet and block of wood—the exposed projections on the corner pieces will slot into the side framing sections already fitted. Push two plastic glides or runners into the lower channel of each bottom framing section and secure them with self-tapping screws.

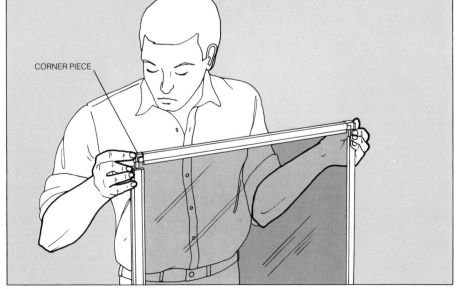

CORNER PIECE

6 **Positioning the sliding frames.** Cut two pieces of running track to the length of the bottom track and fit them into the track channels. Slide draught-seal strips into the appropriate slots on all framing sections—these should face towards the existing window on all sections except the vertical inner sections of frames in the rear channel. Slot each framed pane first into its channel in the top track, and then let it drop gently down into the bottom track.

Fitting a Hinged Frame

Attaching the secondary window. Ensure that there is sufficient width of flat wood on all sides of the window frame to accommodate the fixings; if the frame is metal, or if it has a narrow moulding, secure timber battens to the reveal. Take measurements for the glass pane according to the manufacturer's instructions, cut the glass, and fit the gaskets and framing sections as for a sliding window *(page 73, Steps 4–5)*. With the screws provided, attach hinge pins to one side or the top of the existing window frame, and secure hinge sockets in the groove on the outside of the relevant framing section. Attach turn-catches to the three remaining sides of the existing frame, then hang the secondary pane by slotting the hinge sockets over the pins *(right)*.

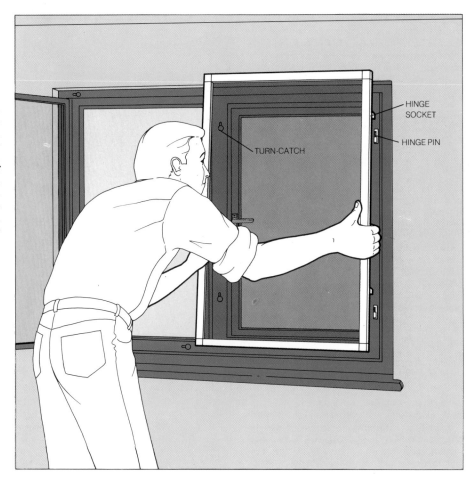

HINGE SOCKET

HINGE PIN

TURN-CATCH

Installing a Sealed Unit

Sealed double-glazed units, which are sometimes known as insulating glass, are installed in much the same way as single panes of glass. Because of their extra weight, however, it is important to place setting blocks along the rebate before inserting the glass—the blocks support the unit and keep it at right angles, so preventing the frame from sagging or jamming.

Sealed units are available in standard sizes or can be specially ordered. For a frame with a narrow rebate that cannot accommodate the extra pane of glass, choose a unit with a stepped edge—that is, with the inner pane of glass slightly larger all round than the outer pane, so that it fits over and not into the rebate.

The first task in installing sealed units is to prepare the frame: remove old glass, glazing sprigs and putty as described on pages 34–35, and prime the rebate. To bed the unit, use a non-hardening compound that will allow the surrounding frame to move slightly without cracking the glass. Take care not to damage the seal between the two glass panes.

1 **Positioning the setting blocks.** Hold a lump of non-hardening putty in one hand and, pressing it out with your thumb, line the rebate to a depth of at least 5 mm. Place metal or plastic setting blocks at quarter points along the frame rebate; the number of blocks required and their correct location vary according to the type of window *(inset)*.

FIXED LIGHT

SIDE-HUNG SASH

TOP-HUNG SASH

PIVOTED SASH

2 **Fitting the unit.** Clean the sealed unit edges with a dry cloth. With a helper, press the unit gently but firmly into the putty, taking care not to dislodge the setting blocks. Secure the unit with glazing sprigs tapped into the rebate with a pin hammer or the side of a chisel blade *(page 38)*.

3 **Sealing the unit.** Seal the inside edge of the unit with non-hardening putty, or, as here, with a strip of foam rubber and wooden beads nailed to the rebate. Nails must be countersunk and the holes filled. Scrape off any excess putty on the outside of the unit with a wet knife.

The Changing Face of Windows: New Materials, New Designs

A new window—either to replace an old one or to fit a new opening in an external wall—can have a considerable effect on the appearance, security and running costs of your home. In order to choose the right window for your specific needs, a basic knowledge of the new construction materials and designs available is essential.

Timber still remains the least expensive construction material for all windows, but, despite improvements in design, the paintwork on softwood windows and the stain or varnish on hardwood windows still require regular attention.

Aluminium windows are available with a natural untreated mill finish, with a pigmented or transparent anodized finish, or with an acrylic paint coating that has been baked on. In its untreated state, aluminium reacts with oxygen in the air to form a protective oxide coating, but the metal may still become discoloured or roughened over a period of time. Both paint and anodized finishes increase the resistance of the metal to weathering and pollution. To maintain their appearance, all aluminium finishes should be wiped down every few months with a non-alkaline detergent and warm water applied with a sponge or soft cloth; abrasive cleaners should not be used. The main disadvantage of aluminium as a construction material for windows is its poor insulating quality, which makes windows susceptible to condensation; for this reason, aluminium is often used in combination with plastic or timber.

White plastic windows are made of uPVC (unplasticized polyvinyl chloride) and incorporate an ultra-violet light stabilizer that prevents discoloration. As with untreated aluminium, a thin oxide coating is formed by the reaction of uPVC with oxygen in the air, and cleaning should be carried out with a mild detergent and a soft cloth or sponge to avoid damage to this oxide coating. With good insulating qualities and the ability to reduce condensation, uPVC is a good choice of construction material but is more expensive than both timber and aluminium.

Almost all modern windows are available in aluminium and uPVC as well as timber, and usually incorporate a number of fittings designed to improve security, draught-proofing and access for cleaning. Weatherstripping seals on opening sashes, and double glazing in the form of sealed units, are standard features. Modern versions of the traditional vertical sliding sash window have spiral balances in place of pulleys and weights, and special release catches allow the sashes to be tilted inwards for easy cleaning. On both side-hung and top-hung casement windows, access for cleaning may be provided by projecting hinges, which allow the outside of the glass to be reached through the gap between sash and frame; on horizontal pivoted windows, release catches allow the sash to be swung completely round into the room. Other design features worth looking out for include catches that can be locked securely and friction hinges that hold the sash open at any angle.

The most sophisticated modern window design is the tilt-and-turn window (opposite page, above), which is relatively new to Britain but which has been in common use in Europe for over two decades. Also introduced from Europe is the external roller blind (opposite page, centre), which retracts into a casing above the window and is usually fitted as an integral part of the window installation. A horizontal pivoted casement window specially designed for sloping roofs is fitted with external cladding and an integral vent-flap (opposite page, below); the installation of this window is shown on pages 82–83.

Unless they significantly alter the appearance of your house, replacement windows do not normally require planning permission. However, any structural alteration you intend to make in one of the house walls, for example making a new opening, may need building regulations approval. The minimum area of ventilation openings required for any room is also determined by building regulations.

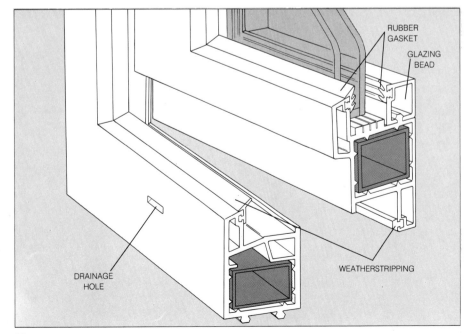

A reinforced uPVC window. Both the sash and the glazing are framed by hollow, multi-chambered profiles of uPVC welded together. The frames are reinforced by steel or aluminium members within the profiles. The double-glazed sealed unit in the sash is held by rubber gaskets and snap-in glazing beads that can easily be removed if the glass needs to be replaced. Flexible weatherstripping seals out draughts between the sash and the main frame.

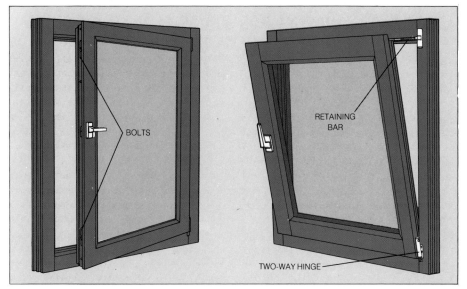

A tilt-and-turn window. This window is hinged both along the bottom and at one side, and opens inwards. It can be swung fully open on the side hinges *(far left)* or tilted slightly open on the bottom hinges and held by the retaining bar for draught-free ventilation *(left)*. A single handle is used both to lock the window and adjust the hinges from swing to tilt; the hinges are often concealed in rebates along the sides of the frame.

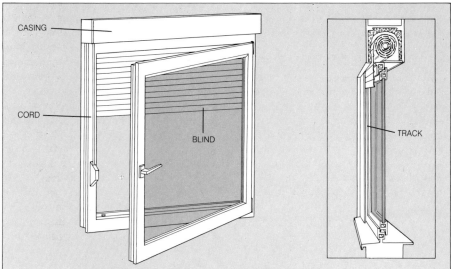

A casement window with roller blind. Installed as an integral part of a side-hung casement window that opens into the room, the lintel casing that houses the roller blind is the same thickness as the wall and extends about 100 mm on each side of the window. The blind is raised and lowered by a spring-balanced cord, and is guided by aluminium, timber or plastic tracks on either side of the external window reveal *(inset)*. The bottom slat of the blind is usually reinforced and is fitted with stops that prevent the blind from disappearing into the casing when it is retracted; the remaining slats are usually plastic.

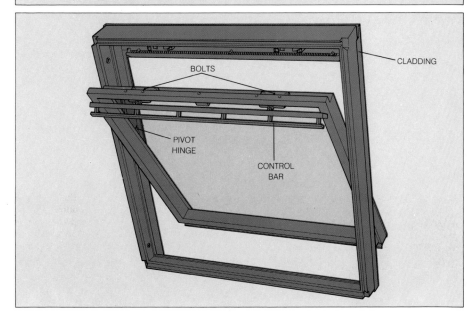

A pivoted roof window. A horizontal control bar is used to open and close both the sash and a ventilation flap concealed between the sash and the main frame. Friction pivot hinges hold the sash securely open at any angle, and also allow the sash to be swung round for cleaning of the outside. The exterior of the window is protected by aluminium cladding.

A Factory-Made Unit, Complete with All Its Parts

In some ways, adding a new window to a room is like hanging a painting or print: it can offer a pleasing view, decorate an empty wall or brighten a drab area. Of course, a window can do more than that: it can let light and fresh air into the house.

Once you have cut a rough opening (*pages 54–57 and 61–65*), or removed an old window that you want to replace (*pages 66–67*), installing such a window takes only a few hours—thanks to prefabricated or pre-hung units. A pre-hung timber window comes complete with the sashes, jambs and sill, and with the hardware needed to open and lock the sashes; the sashes and fixed lights come unglazed, and must be fitted with glass or double-glazed sealed units after the window has been installed.

In addition to built-in conveniences such as these, the windows come in a range of designs and materials. Aluminium windows are usually screwed to a timber sub-frame which is installed in the same way as a pre-hung timber frame. Windows constructed of uPVC generally need to be fitted by the supplier. Internal window

boards for all pre-hung windows must be bought and fitted separately.

If the sill of the timber frame does not project at least 30 mm beyond the wall, you will need to chip out more brickwork at the bottom of the opening and install a concrete sub-sill (*Steps 1–2*). To prevent water penetrating the joint between the sub-sill and the timber frame, a galvanized steel water bar should be bedded into grooves along the top of the sub-sill and the underside of the timber frame (*Step 3*).

To secure the jambs of the pre-hung timber frame to the wall, use special screws pre-fitted with sleeves (*page 80, Step 5*); these fixings allow the window to be secured in the wall without having to be removed and repositioned after plugs have been inserted. Box-frame sliding sash windows are secured just with wedges at the top and bottom (*page 81*).

Rebated openings (*page 60*) are not necessary for casement windows or for modern sliding sash windows with spiral balances, but are preferred by many professionals because they protect the window

frame from the effects of sun and rain and also because they improve the weatherproofing of the joint between the frame and the wall. Traditional box-frame sliding sash windows, whose wide linings, containing pulleys, cords and weights, take up more space than the jambs of casement windows, should always be installed in a rebated opening (*page 81*).

Before deciding on any window unit, refer to manufacturers' catalogues. Note the rough opening sizes required for the pre-hung windows you are considering, and check them against your available space. Check the availability of double glazing, weatherproofing and the other features described on page 76. When ordering casement windows, specify the direction in which the sashes must swing.

One final caution: some pre-hung windows are assembled for use in new construction while others are designed for openings in existing walls. The installation techniques shown here apply to the second category alone; do not use them with a unit meant for new construction.

Installing the Window

1 **Preparing the opening.** Using a club hammer and a cold chisel, chip out brickwork at the bottom of the wall opening to make way for the pre-cast sub-sill and its stooled ends (*pages 58–59*). The sub-sill should overhang the edge of the wall by at least 30 mm. Prepare a batch of mortar: mix sand and cement in proportions of 4 to 1, then dissolve a plasticizer in water according to manufacturer's instructions and add this to the sand and cement until the mortar acquires a workable consistency. Lay the mortar along the bottom of the wall opening with a bricklayer's trowel (*right*).

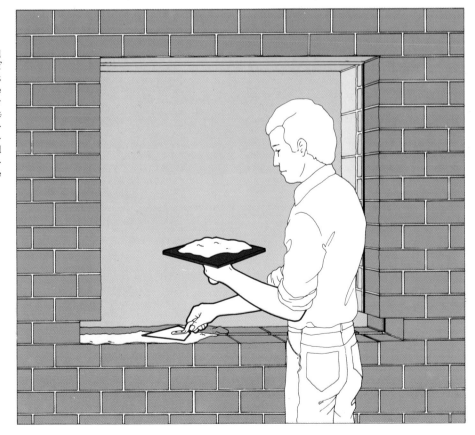

2 **Bedding the sill in the wall.** With the aid of a helper, lift the pre-cast sub-sill into position on the wall, bedding it firmly down on the mortar. Check that the sill is correctly aligned with the wall, and then use a spirit level to check that it is horizontal; if necessary, insert fragments of slate or other packing material underneath the sub-sill. If the sill does not extend across the full thickness of the wall, lay a course of bricks to raise the inside of the wall to the level of the sill. Leave the mortar to set overnight.

3 **Fitting a water bar.** Cut a length of 19 by 6mm galvanized steel bar to the width of the wall opening. Lay mortar or spread mastic in the groove running along the top of the sub-sill, then bed the water bar in the groove *(right)*. Prepare the new window unit for installation by spreading mastic in the groove for the water bar along the underside of the frame.

GALVANIZED STEEL BAR

4 **Positioning the window unit.** If the new window frame has projecting horns at the ends of the rails, square these round and saw them off. Lift the window unit into position and secure it in the opening with wedges at the top and bottom *(right)*. Check that the window is plumb and level; insert packing where necessary between the jambs and the edges of the wall. Mark positions for two or three fixings in each jamb, aligning the marks with the exposed edges of bricks and not with the mortar joints between them.

WEDGES

5 **Securing the window.** At each pencil mark on the jambs, drill through the jamb rebate and into the wall to the depth specified by the fixing manufacturer. Check that the window is still plumb and that the sashes open and close smoothly. Press a jamb fixing, with its sleeve, firmly into each hole, then drive in the fixings with a screwdriver. Cover the screw heads with wooden plugs or with special caps supplied with the fixings.

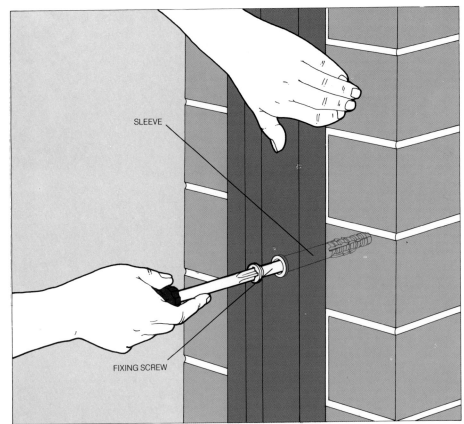

SLEEVE

FIXING SCREW

6 **Sealing the joints.** Working from both sides of the wall—or, in a rebated opening, from the inside only—press mortar into the gaps between the window frame and the edges of the wall opening. Leave the mortar to set, then seal the joints between the frame and the wall on the outside with mastic sealant *(above)*.

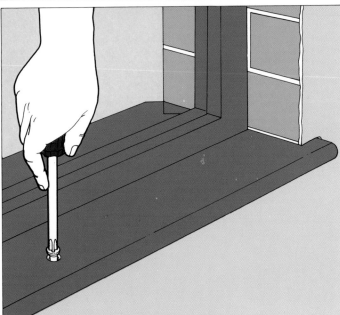

7 **Attaching a window board.** Slot the rear tongue of the window board into the corresponding groove in the fitted window frame; if desired, the joint can be strengthened with nails driven diagonally through the board into the frame, and then covered with quadrant moulding. To secure the window board firmly in the reveal, drill down through the centre of the board and into the wall, then drive in a screw *(above)*. Cover the screw head with filler or a wooden plug.

8 **Completing the installation.** Make good the internal plasterwork round the frame and beneath the window board, using a timber board to protect the surface of the fitted frame as you apply the plaster. With a steel float, smooth the plaster flush with the wall surface. Glaze the fixed lights and opening sashes of the window with single panes of glass *(pages 36–38)* or double-glazed sealed units *(page 75)*.

Installing a Box-Frame Sash Window in a Rebated Opening

Knocking in wedges. Lift the pre-hung window unit into position in the opening; press it firmly against the edges of the rebate. Check that the window is plumb, then secure it by knocking in wedges between the lining head and the lintel and between the bottom of the frame and the sub-sill or wall. Fill any gaps between the sides of the frame and the wall with mortar. Seal the external joint between the frame and the wall with mastic. Attach the window board and make good the internal plaster as for a casement window. If the inside of the frame is flush with the wall, attach architraves down the sides and along the top of the window as described on pages 24–27.

WEDGE

Putting In a Skylight That Opens

A ready-made skylight is the simplest way of ventilating and lighting a roof space; it can also serve as an emergency exit. Today's units, most of which swing through 180 degrees for easy cleaning, are ready glazed with double or triple glazing, and come with flashing to suit different roof coverings. Those for roofs with a slope of less than 20 degrees have their own wedge-shaped frames to increase the slope of the window. Rods, cords or electric motors are available to open inaccessible windows.

Both the making of the roof opening *(pages 68–69)* and the installation of the window can usually be done from inside. To finish the opening, you must insert trimmers top and bottom, nailing them to the side framing rafters and the ends of the cut intermediate rafters. When only one rafter is cut, you can use timber of the same dimensions for the trimmers; if cutting two or more rafters, you should increase the thickness of the trimmers by 25 mm. If the window frame is too narrow to span the gap between the rafters exactly, install a false rafter to create a gap of the correct width. When the opening is ready, the window frame can be installed and weatherproofed following the manufacturer's instructions.

Finally, the tiles will have to be replaced up to the flashing round the frame. Cut tiles to fit at both the sides and the top; at the bottom of the frame, the flashing will cover the gap between the frame and the top of the first run of tiles. Clay tiles can be scored and broken, but you will need an angle grinder for concrete ones. To support the short tile course above the window, install a tilting fillet—a strip of soft metal that runs over the top flashing. This is usually supplied as part of the window kit.

1 **Installing the trimmers.** Cut a hole in the roof following the instructions given on pages 68–69. Measure the distance between the two side framing rafters at the top and bottom of the opening. Cut two trimmers from timber the same dimensions as the rafters, to fit the measured spans. (If more than one rafter has been cut, use trimmers 25 mm thicker than the rafters.) Fix a trimmer in position at the top of the opening by nailing through it into the cut end of each rafter, then nail through the side framing rafters into the trimmer ends. Install the bottom trimmer in the same way. For standard 100 by 50 mm rafters, use 100 mm round-wire nails.

2 **Putting in a false rafter.** Measure the external width of the window frame and, starting at the side framing rafter, measure this distance on each trimmer. Cut a false rafter to fit between the trimmers; fix the rafter in place by nailing through the trimmers into its ends. Nail the battens to the false rafter, and trim them flush with it if necessary.

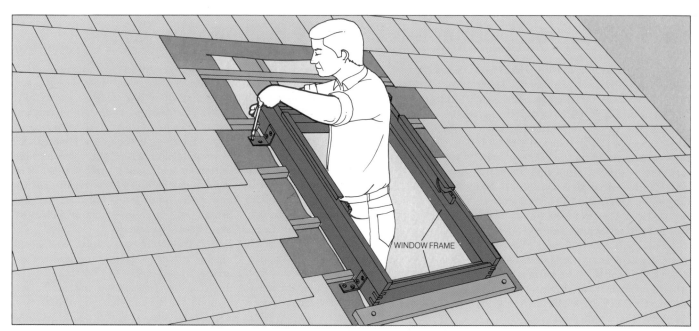

WINDOW FRAME

3 **Securing the window frame.** At the bottom of the opening nail a piece of wood across the rafters to create a temporary spacer bar. The timber for this should be as wide as the recommended distance between the window frame and the roof covering. Then set the window frame in position, resting it on the spacer bar. Using only a single screw in the top left and lower right brackets, fix the window frame temporarily to the rafters. Make sure that the frame is perfectly square by carefully checking that the internal diagonal measurements are equal. Then screw the window frame to the rafters using all four brackets, and remove the spacer bar.

FLASHING

4 **Finishing the window.** Fit the flashing, following the manufacturer's instructions. Then replace the tiles so that they overlap the flashing at the sides and the top of the frame. Working upwards from the bottom of the frame, slide each tile with its nib over the batten under its neighbour, so that it locks into place; trim tiles to fit, using an angle grinder if necessary. Nail the side tiles to the battens as you go *(left)*. At the top of the frame install a tilting fillet and rehang the top tiles; make sure that the short course above the window rests evenly on the fillet. Finally, install the window in the frame, according to the instructions.

The Flat-Roofed Dormer—a Window Built into the Roof

A dormer that is built into a roof can bring sunlight and fresh air to a dim and stuffy attic. It can form the starting point for a new room, and thus add to the capacity and value of your home. And, with one type at least, it is something that you can build yourself without too much difficulty.

A dormer window stretching the entire length of a roof needs professional planning. But constructing two or more flat-roofed dormers of the kind shown below does not call for the specialized skill of an architect. Basically, the work consists of three jobs of carpentry: cutting an opening in the existing roof, fitting a frame into the opening, and then installing a window in the front wall of the frame. Covering the frame with roofing felt and flashings is a job normally left to a professional.

Installing a dormer as part of a roof conversion requires careful research and planning. First you must ensure that your roof is suitable for modification—a trussed roof, for instance, cannot be altered. In some roofs the headroom may be insufficient, and in most cases the floor will need strengthening. Points relating to the minimum height of the window, light and ventilation, the proximity to party walls, chimneys and vent pipes, access, insulation and fireproofing must all be considered. Check building regulations with your local authority planning department.

Plan the dormer itself in a detailed scale drawing on graph paper, showing exactly where the roof opening for it will be cut. Then submit your proposal to the local authority for approval. Once approval has been received, the plan can be used to draw up an accurate shopping list.

For the construction work, you will need pieces of 100 by 50 mm timber, many of which must be cut at precise angles marked out with a sliding bevel or, for right angles, a try square. For the cladding on the roof and cheeks you will need to buy pre-felted chipboard or exterior-grade plywood. Oil-tempered hardboard is an alternative cladding for use on the cheeks only. If you are using hardboard or plywood, buy roofing felt to cover the cheeks before fastening the fascia boards. The choice of the window itself is a matter of personal preference and price, but look for one whose exterior panes can easily be cleaned from inside the dormer.

Before starting work, place a roof ladder on either side of the opening, and place a scaffold plank below it. For extra safety, erect a platform tower or scaffolding against the wall in line with the dormer. Cordon off the area at ground level and erect signs warning that there is work in progress overhead. Have sheets of polythene at hand to cover the opening at night, and in case of rain.

Anatomy of a dormer. The skeleton of a flat-roofed dormer consists entirely of 100 by 50 mm timbers. At the sides, this skeleton is supported by reinforced rafters in the existing roof. The front wall is supported by reinforced corner posts standing on a sole plate nailed to the attic floor. Trimmers at the top and bottom of the dormer close the roof opening. Layer boards beneath the tiles define the edges of the structure and provide fixing surfaces for flashing. Cross ceiling joists are nailed between two side ceiling joists running from the front wall to the top of the reinforcing rafters. Cheek studs, cross ceiling joists and tapered battens across the cross ceiling joists provide fixing points for the covering and interior plasterboard finish. Cripple studs below the window opening complete the frame.

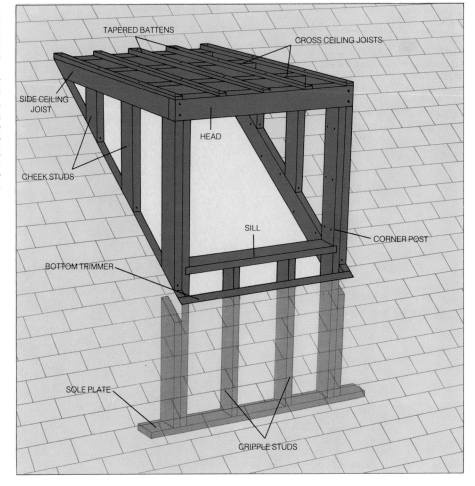

1 **Putting in the trimmers.** Following the plans you have drawn up, cut an opening in the roof *(pages 68–69)*. Cut two trimmers from timber the same size as the rafters—usually 100 by 50 mm—to fit between the two side framing rafters. Using 100 mm round-wire nails, nail a trimmer to the ends of the cut rafters at the bottom and top of the opening. Then secure the trimmers with two nails, driven into the end of each trimmer through a side rafter.

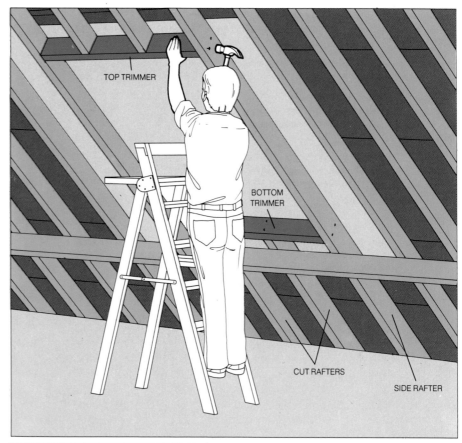

TOP TRIMMER

BOTTOM TRIMMER

CUT RAFTERS

SIDE RAFTER

2 **Reinforcing the side rafters.** Using timber the same size as the existing rafters, cut two reinforcing rafters to fit between the top and bottom trimmers. Position them against the side rafters and clamp them. Secure them to the rafters with 100 mm round-wire nails staggered at 300 mm intervals *(right)*.

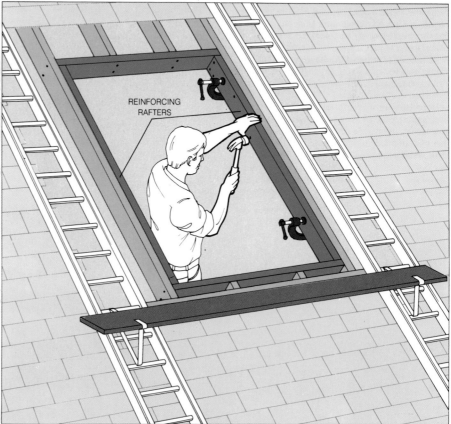

REINFORCING RAFTERS

3 **Making reinforcing sections for corner posts.** Cut a sole plate from 100 by 50 mm timber about 300 mm longer than the width of the dormer. Nail it to the floor directly below the bottom trimmer so that it extends equally beyond each side. Cut a piece of 100 by 50 mm timber a little more than the height of the finished dormer above the floor. Rest it on the sole plate, holding it vertically against the reinforcing rafter and bottom trimmer, then mark off the top and bottom edges of the rafter on to the timber *(right)*. Cut along the marks to make upper and lower reinforcing sections for the corner post. Prepare reinforcing sections for the other corner post in the same way.

4 **Fixing the corner posts.** Cut two lengths of 100 by 50 mm timber slightly longer than the height of the finished dormer, to form the corner posts. Stand one post vertically on the sole plate against a reinforcing rafter and the bottom trimmer. Using two 100 mm nails, fix it to the reinforcing rafter and toenail its base to the sole plate. Fix the other post in the same way. Stand the appropriate upper reinforcing section on the reinforcing rafter, against the corner post, and clamp it in position. Nail it to the corner post with three pairs of 100 mm nails. Place the lower reinforcing section on the sole plate and against the corner post beneath the reinforcing rafter; secure it to the corner post in the same way, toenailing it to the sole plate. Reinforce the second corner post using the same method.

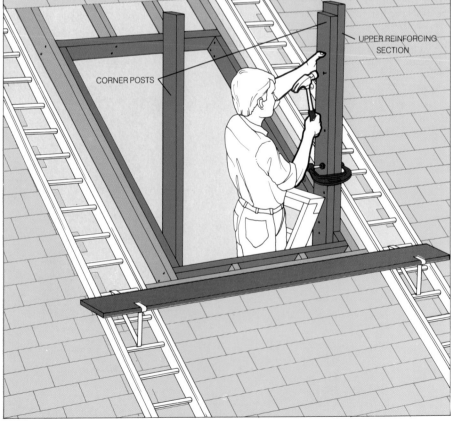

5 **Trimming off the corner posts.** Cut a piece of 100 by 50 mm timber about 250 mm longer than the depth of the dormer roof—it can be used later as a side ceiling joist. Rest one end on the top trimmer and the other against the corner post. Check that it is horizontal, using a spirit level *(right)*. Mark the corner post where the bottom edge of the piece of timber crosses it and square the mark round the corner post and reinforcing section. Mark the other corner post in the same way. Then cut each corner post and reinforcing section off at the mark, using a handsaw.

6 **Putting on the head.** Saw a length of 100 by 50 mm timber to fit between the outside edges of the double corner posts. Turning the timber on edge as shown, position it on top of the corner posts so that it is flush with their front sides. With a helper holding the timber steady, toenail it in position at each end.

7 **Fixing the side ceiling joists.** Place the piece of timber used in Step 5 to mark the corner posts on edge, with one end on the corner post butting against the head, and the other resting on the top trimmer. Fix the front end to the head using two 100 mm round-wire nails, then secure the other end to the side rafter with two 100 mm nails. Install the other side ceiling joist in the same way. Inside the roof, trim the side ceiling joists diagonally so that they are flush with the rafters.

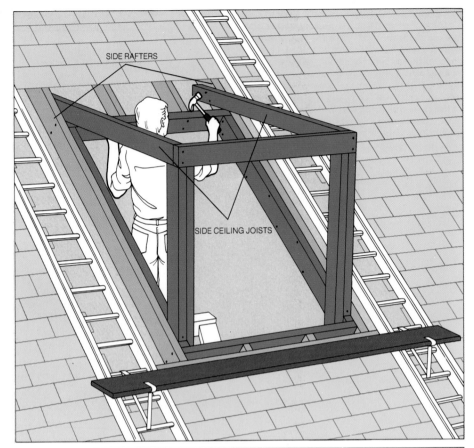

SIDE RAFTERS

SIDE CEILING JOISTS

8 **Inserting the sill.** Take an inside measurement between the corner posts, add 20 mm, and cut a 100 by 50 mm piece of timber to this length. Hold it against the corner posts at the height of the planned sill, with the 100 mm side facing upwards. Check that it is level and outline the 10 mm overlap on either side on to each corner post. Remove the timber, saw into the posts along the marks, and carefully chisel out notches; work from the outer edges towards the centre to avoid splitting the wood *(right)*. Slide the sill into the notches and toenail it in position.

Measure the distance between the underside of the sill and the sole plate and cut two pieces of timber to fit, to form cripple studs. Space the studs evenly on the sole plate between the corner posts *(inset)* and fix them in position: nail through the sill at the top and toenail at the base.

SILL

CRIPPLE STUDS

SOLE PLATE

9 **Fitting the cross ceiling joists.** Measure the distance between the inside edges of the side ceiling joists. Cut three pieces of 100 by 50 mm timber to this length. Mark fixing positions for each cross ceiling joist on to the side ceiling joists; site them at 400 mm centres. With a helper holding a cross ceiling joist in position, drive two 100 mm nails through each side ceiling joist into the ends of the cross ceiling joist; you will have to work outside on the roof to do this. Install the other two cross ceiling joists in the same way.

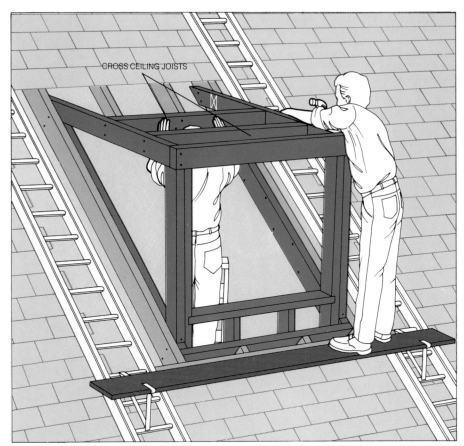

10 **Installing the cheek studs.** Mark positions for the cheek studs on the side ceiling joists: the studs should be equally spaced, at a maximum of 400 mm centres. Hold a length of 100 by 50 mm timber against one of the side ceiling joists and the side of the reinforcing rafter at the first mark. Check that it is vertical, then mark the stud horizontally where it meets the side ceiling joist, and diagonally where it meets the reinforcing rafter. Saw through the stud at the marks. Place the stud between the side ceiling joist and the reinforcing rafter and toenail it in place. Install the other cheek studs in the same way.

11 **Cladding the cheeks.** Measure the sides of the triangle formed by the side ceiling joists, the front edge of the corner post reinforcement section, and the reinforcing rafter. Transfer the measurements on to a sheet of cladding material. Cut out the sheet and fix it in place using 50 mm galvanized nails at 150 mm intervals. Cut and fix the other cheek cladding in the same way.

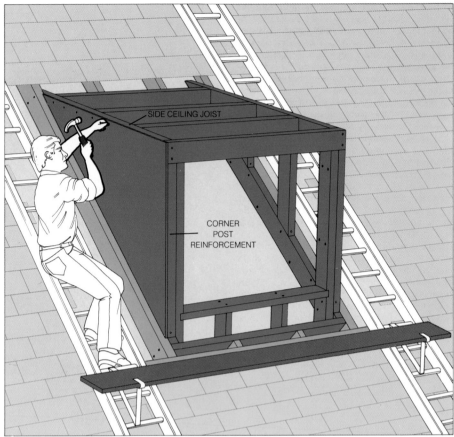

12 **Installing the decking.** Measure the width of the dormer roof, divide this figure by 300 mm to determine the number of tapered battens required. To make tapered battens, cut pieces of 50 by 50 mm timber to the depth of the roof. At one end of each 50 by 50, make a mark 10 mm from the top edge; at the other end make a mark 10 mm from the bottom edge. Join the two marks on either side of the strip to make two diagonal lines *(inset)*; cut along the lines to make two tapered battens. Place a tapered batten on top of the side ceiling joist flush with the cheek, with its thicker end to the back of the dormer and its right-angled corner downwards. Nail it in position using 75 mm round-wire nails at 300 mm intervals. Fix a tapered batten on to the other side ceiling joist in the same way. Position the remaining tapered battens, parallel to the first two, across the cross ceiling joists at 300 mm centres. Fix them to the cross ceiling joists and the head at 300 mm intervals, using 75 mm round-wire nails at the wider end and 50 mm round-wire nails at the thinner end.

Cut a square of exterior-grade plywood or prefelted chipboard to the area of the roof. Fix it in place by driving 50 mm galvanized nails through the tapered battens at 150 mm intervals.

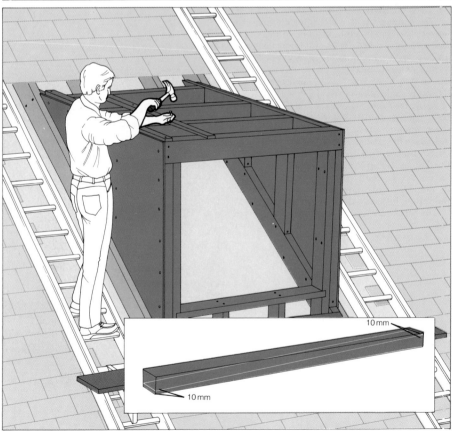

13 **Securing layer boards and fascia boards.** To make the layer boards, cut two lengths of 225 by 25 mm timber the same width as the dormer. Place one piece on the main roof above the dormer, with its bottom edge butting against the back edge of the roof decking, and fix it in position using 50 mm galvanized nails. Place the other piece on the main roof immediately below the dormer, butting against the corner posts, and secure it in the same way as before. Then measure the distance between the outer edges of the top and bottom layer boards, and cut two pieces of 225 by 25 mm timber to this length. Position one on either side of the dormer, hard against the cheeks, and nail them in position.

To make the first side fascia, cut a piece of 150 by 25 mm timber slightly longer than the depth of the dormer roof. Set a sliding bevel to the angle between the roof decking and the side layer board. Transfer this angle to one corner of the piece you have just sawn, and cut to shape. Position the side fascia over the top of the cheek cladding; fix it to the side ceiling joist behind with two rows of 50 mm lost-head nails at 150 mm intervals. Make and fix the other side fascia in the same way. Trim the side fascia boards flush with the front wall, if necessary. For the front fascia, cut a length of 150 by 25 mm timber to the full width of the dormer. Position it at the top of the front wall and fix it to the head in the same way as before, using 37 mm oval nails at the corners to fix into the two side fascia boards.

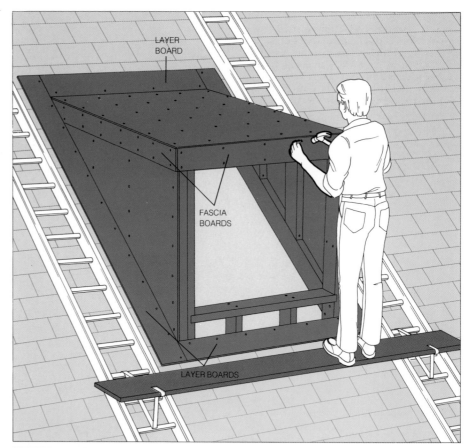

14 **Attaching tilt fillets and a drip batten.** Using 50 by 50 mm angled timber, cut two pieces slightly longer than the depth of the dormer roof. Measure the angle between the top layer board and the dormer roof with a sliding bevel. Transfer this angle to the angled timber and saw along the marks. Using 50 mm galvanized nails, fix the right angle of each piece flush with the edge of a side fascia, to make tilt fillets. Trim off the front ends flush with the front fascia, angling them slightly inwards.

Make a drip batten by cutting a piece of 50 by 25 mm timber slightly longer than the width of the dormer. Using 50 mm galvanized nails, fix it flush with the top of the front fascia, with the 25 mm side facing upwards. Cut off the ends of the batten flush with the side fascia *(right)*.

The dormer should now be weatherproofed and roofed by a professional before you install your window *(pages 78–81)*.

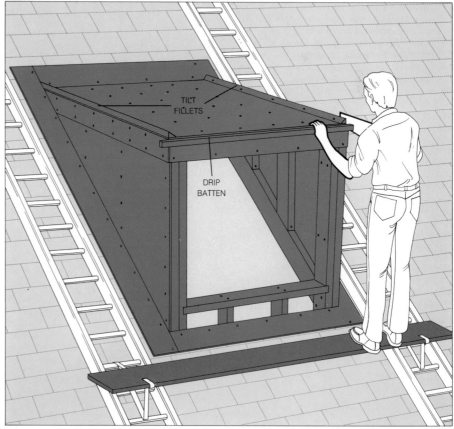

4 A Door for Every Purpose

Handcrafting a door lining. A length of timber, cut to the width of the door opening, rests on its edge behind one of the two jambs that will form the sides of a lining for an internal door. The projecting tongue on the jamb will slot into the corresponding housing cut in the end of the lining head. A recess in the inner face of the jamb has been cut with the bevel-edged chisel; the hinge leaves will be set into recesses in both the door and the jamb and secured with the wood screws.

If you go shopping for a door these days you may be in for some surprises. Over the last decade or two, door-makers have revolutionized their product with new materials, designs and methods of manufacture. Old stereotypes—a door is always heavy, always made of wood, always installed by painstaking custom craftsmanship—no longer apply. A modern interior flush door, for instance, is very likely to have a lightweight inner filling of paperboard or extruded chipboard, and—as with windows—aluminium and plastic (uPVC) are now employed as construction materials for both doors and their frames.

The greatest revolution of all has taken place in the form in which a door is generally delivered for installation. Traditionally, a door was installed by the most skilful carpenter in a builder's crew. The job called for precise fitting to close tolerances, and every part but the door itself, from the jigsaw puzzle of lining, stops and architraves to the holes for locks and bolts, was fashioned by hand. Today, that work is done at the factory. A prefabricated—or, to use the language of modern carpentry, pre-hung—door is transported as a complete unit, with the frame components, pre-cut and pre-drilled for assembly, the door hinged and mounted, and the lock holes cut. The entire unit, levelled and plumbed, is simply screwed into a wall opening—a job that takes, at most, a couple of hours, and one that a beginner can do almost as easily as a veteran craftsman *(pages 94–96)*.

The idea of the "pre-hung" has spread to every kind of door manufacture, and the range of models increases almost every year. Once designed as conventional interior doors, pre-hungs now come in specialized designs for special purposes. Some are features of modern home building—a sliding, floor-to-ceiling set of glass doors, for example, links a living room to a patio or garden. Garage doors that roll in sections on overhead tracks or that swing upwards to the garage roof *(pages 116–123)* can take the place of side-hung doors that sagged under their own weight and dragged against the ground. And in addition to the ever-increasing range of styles, a variety of features designed to improve sound and thermal insulation is now incorporated as standard fittings in many pre-hung doors: draught-proofing strips and external weather bars are often factory-installed, and exterior doors and frames may have rebates along the side and top edges.

Meanwhile, the craftsman's tradition of hanging a door from scratch is far from ended. For all their versatility, pre-hung doors do not come in every style or size, and an odd-sized opening must still be fitted with a frame and door in the old-fashioned way *(pages 98–107)*. An antique door, acquired for its beauty or associations, cannot be installed in any other way because its frame must be assembled on the spot. Such a job is a demanding one, but once the basic skills of accurate measurement and cutting are mastered, and the sequence of procedures understood, it, too, becomes routine.

Pre-Hung Units for Easy Fitting

A pre-hung door unit for internal walls is the woodworking equivalent of a ready-to-wear suit. The most difficult part of the work is done in a factory—the jambs and lining head are pre-cut and pre-drilled for assembly, the door is hinged and the lock is installed. You do the final fitting; assembling the components, setting the unit snugly into a new rough opening *(Chapter 2)* or an old opening formerly occupied by a door you have discarded, and fastening the lining to the wall with screws.

Although the principle of easy assembly applies to all door sets, the design of the different components, and the way they fit together, varies according to the individual manufacturer. Some door set kits comprise a door with fitted latch and lock, three sections of lining with hinges attached and six separate sections of mitred architrave; in other kits, such as the one shown here, the lining sections and door-side architraves are single units, and the remaining architraves are assembled and then slotted into grooves in the fitted lining.

Before buying a door set, measure the height and width of the opening, and also the thickness of the wall. The standard height of an internal flush door is usually 1981 mm (2030 mm in Australia); standard widths are 610, 686 and 762 mm. Door set linings are available in a range of depths appropriate to different wall thicknesses. Decide on which side of the wall the door is to open, and whether it is to open to the left or the right.

The most important stage in the installation of a door set—and the one most dependent on your own skill—is positioning the lining correctly in the wall opening. If the lining is leaning slightly to one side, or is not exactly plumb, the door will not open and close properly—and you cannot then plane a veneered door to fit without damaging its appearance. Always attend first to the hinge side of the lining *(Step 2, opposite page)*; once this jamb has been correctly aligned and packed out, it is a relatively simple matter to adjust the lining head and opposite jamb as necessary.

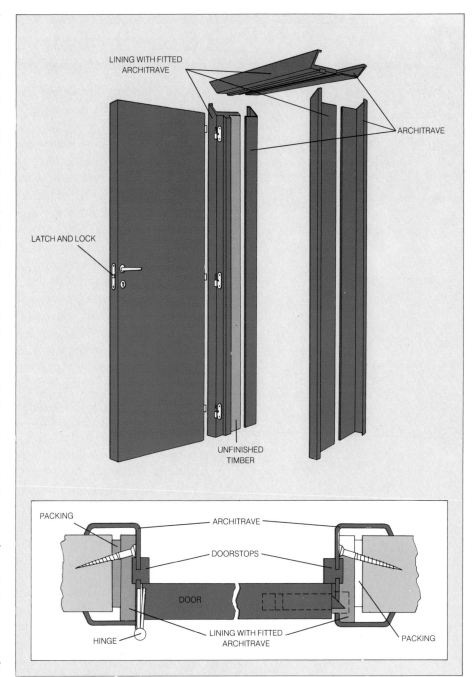

Components of a door set. This door set kit comprises three sections of combined lining and door-side architrave, with fitted doorstop and hinge pins; three separate sections of architrave; and a door with hinges, latch and lock. On the combined lining and architrave sections, the architrave and doorstop are faced with a lacquered veneer; the remaining portion of the lining is rough, unfinished timber. The lining is screwed to the wall through the unfinished timber, and the separate, veneered, sections of architrave are then slotted into grooves in the doorstop to cover the rough timber *(inset)*. Handles and handle plates must be bought separately.

1 **Assembling the lining.** Slot the three combined lining and door-side architrave sections together by sliding the plastic guides on the jambs into the corresponding guides on the lining head. Push the components firmly together until the corners are correctly aligned, then secure the assembly by inserting the bolts provided through the pre-drilled holes and tightening them.

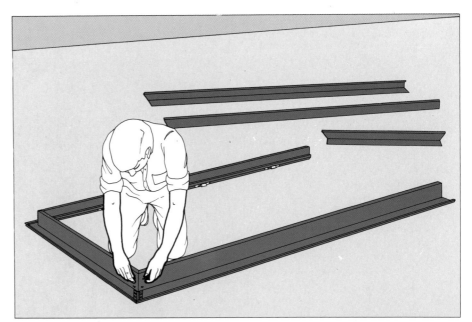

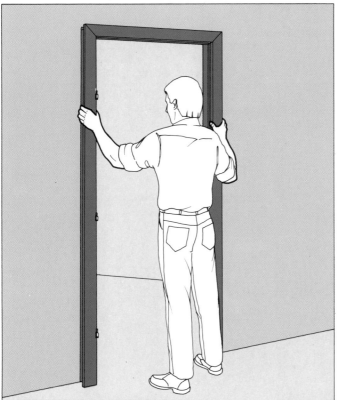

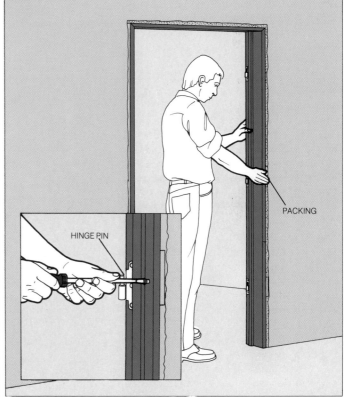

2 **Fitting the lining in the wall.** Position the assembled lining in the wall opening; ensure that the gap between wall and jambs is roughly equal on both sides. Butt the fitted architrave tightly against the wall. Use a long spirit level to check that the hinge-side jamb is plumb and that it is not leaning to one side of the doorway; the flexible architrave profile allows the top or bottom of the jamb to be pulled in slightly if necessary.

3 **Securing the hinge side.** Working on the other side of the doorway, insert packing between the hinge-side jamb and the wall at the height of each of the three hinge pins *(above)*. Drill holes through the unfinished area on the hinge-side jamb at the height of each hinge; if the wall is of block or brick construction, drill into the wall also and insert plugs. Secure the hinge-side jamb to the wall with No. 10 screws long enough to grip both jamb and packing and penetrate the wall by at least 25 mm *(inset)*.

4 **Hanging the door.** Holding the door at right angles to the lining, lower the three hinge sockets attached to the door leaf on to the corresponding hinge pins on the jamb. Attach handles and handle plates to both sides of the door. Close the door, correct the alignment of the unattached jamb, and then insert packing material between the jamb and the wall. Drill through the closing-side jamb at the same heights as on the hinge-side jamb, then secure the unattached jamb to the wall with No. 10 screws.

HINGE SOCKET

HINGE PIN

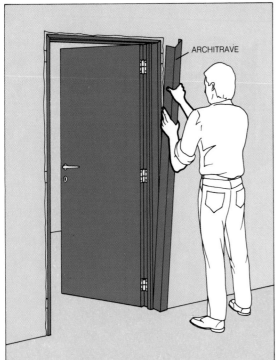

ARCHITRAVE

5 **Trimming the architraves to fit.** Insert the inside edge of one architrave section into the corresponding groove in the doorstop on the fitted lining; if there is a gap between the outer face of the architrave and the wall, trim the inside edge with a smoothing plane until the architrave butts firmly against the wall. Test and trim the other two sections of architrave in the same way.

6 **Securing the architraves.** Slot together and secure the three architrave sections in the same way as the lining sections (page 95, Step 1). Spread PVA glue on the unfinished timber area down the jambs and along the lining head, then slide the architrave assembly into the lining. Press the inside edges of the architraves firmly into the grooves on the fitted lining. Cut three braces from scrap timber to the width of the door opening. Pad the ends of the braces with soft cloth in order to protect the veneer finish on the architraves, then wedge the braces between the glued architrave sections, which will hold the architraves securely in place until the glue has dried.

Choosing the Right Lock

An internal door, which may be fitted with a lock for reasons of convenience and privacy, does not require an expensive high-security lock, but on an exterior door—or the final exit door in a flat—it is essential that the lock bolt can be "deadlocked" so that it can be opened only with a key. The traditional nightlatch lock, which has only a thumb turn and a sliding button on the inside, does not by itself provide any real degree of security.

The two main types of lock are the mortise lock *(right, above)*, which is housed in a mortise cut into the stile of the door, and the cylinder rim lock *(right, below)*, which is mounted on the inside face of the door. Both types are available in a wide range of designs, with a high number of key differs (variations of key design), and with the option of key registration—a scheme under which a new key may only be cut with the owner's authority. Mortise locks with a cylinder mechanism, a combination of the two types, are also available.

A mortise lock may comprise a simple lock body with deadbolt and matching keep plate, or it may include a latchbolt and hole for the doorhandle spindle; to install either design, follow the instructions on pages 104–106. Standard-size mortise locks should not be fitted in a door less than 45 mm thick as the mortise can weaken the stile. For an exterior door, choose a lock with at least five internal levers (which correspond to the notches and projections on the flat-bitted key); for an interior door a two-lever lock is sufficient.

A cylinder lock is operated by a tumbler pin mechanism in place of levers, and for an exterior door should have at least five pins. Fitting instructions are usually enclosed with the lock, together with a paper template for marking the positions for the cylinder hole and screwholes. After the holes have been drilled, the mounting plate, cylinder and lock case are secured to the door with the screws provided by the manufacturer. Cylinders can usually be changed without replacing the whole lock if the key is lost or stolen.

A mortise lock. The latchbolt on this mortise lock is operated by doorhandles and a spindle, and the deadbolt is operated by key. The keep plate is screwed into a recess in the door jamb; on mortise locks for exterior doors, a box-type keep plate may be fitted for extra security, and the deadbolt may have hardened steel rollers that cannot be cut through with a saw.

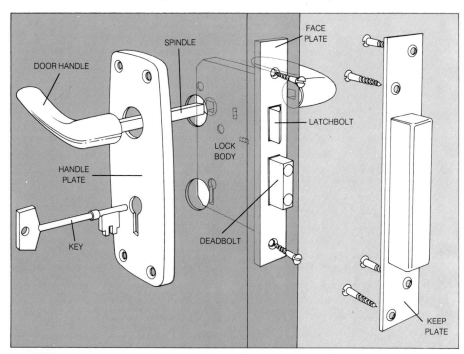

DOOR HANDLE
SPINDLE
FACE PLATE
LATCHBOLT
LOCK BODY
HANDLE PLATE
KEY
DEADBOLT
KEEP PLATE

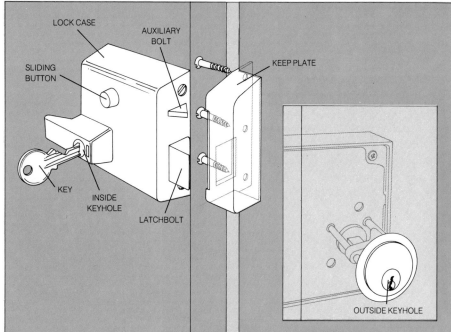

LOCK CASE
AUXILIARY BOLT
KEEP PLATE
SLIDING BUTTON
KEY
INSIDE KEYHOLE
LATCHBOLT
OUTSIDE KEYHOLE

A cylinder deadlatch. This lock, for use on exterior doors, can be deadlocked with a key from both inside the door *(above)* and outside *(inset)*. As the door is closed, the auxiliary bolt is pressed inwards by the keep plate, deadlocking the latchbolt which cannot then be forced open by a piece of card from outside. The inside knob can be locked before you leave the house so that, when the door is closed, both latchbolt and knob are deadlocked; this prevents the door from being opened by any intruder inside the house without a key. The latchbolt can be held back in the lock case by moving the sliding button, and can be locked in that position with the key.

The Fine Art of Fitting and Hanging a Door

A door set consisting of a pre-hung door and its lining *(pages 94–96)* provides an easy way to fill an internal door opening—but not necessarily the best or only way. Sometimes you must hang a door in an existing lining because only the door needs replacing. At other times you must build a new lining because the space available for an opening does not match any factory-made door set. Both jobs call for special preparations and carpentry techniques.

The first job is by far the easier. You must be sure, of course, that the new door will fit the old opening in height, width and thickness: you should be able to find one of matching thickness, but you may have to settle for one that is slightly oversize in height and width, and trim it to fit. Internal doors are usually available in heights of 2032 and 1981 mm (2030 mm in Australia), and in widths of 610 to 838 mm (610 to 820 mm in Australia).

To build a lining for a new opening, order planed-all-round (PAR) timber 30 mm thick whose width is equal to the thickness of the wall plus the plaster covering on both sides. You may need the timber yard to mill pieces of stock to the width you need or trim the stock yourself with a plane.

Assembling and fitting the lining involves fixing the jambs to the lining head with tongue and groove joints, plumbing the lining in the door opening and securing it with screws *(here and overleaf)*. To make the cutting of the grooves easier, the lining head is cut slightly longer than the width of the wall opening; the projecting horns are usually sawn off after the lining has been assembled *(Step 7)*, but on a masonry wall you can remove extra bricks to accommodate them in the wall. When cutting the tongues, be careful; a tongue that is too wide can easily be pared down to fit, but a loose tongue cannot be remedied.

New doors are supplied without any door furniture, so you must cut recesses for the hinges, latch and lock and then attach the handles *(pages 102–106)*. On a hollow-core door, the closing side—which is fitted with an internal block for the mortise latch—is indicated with a stamped mark.

Order the hinges, handles and latch when you buy the door. Two hinges are adequate for most doors, but a heavy door requires three. If the door has to clear a deep-pile carpet as it opens, plane the bottom of the door or install rising-butt hinges; these are attached in the same way as ordinary butt hinges, but the top of the door must be planed at an angle to enable it to clear the lining as it opens *(page 107)*.

For accuracy in measurement, use a combination square and a combined mortise and marking gauge; other tools required are a spirit level, a tenon saw, a smoothing or jack plane, a mallet, and sharp wood chisels of the appropriate size. To hold the door firmly while planing edges or cutting recesses, secure one end in a slot cut into a sawhorse butted against a wall, or construct a purpose-made jack from pieces of scrap timber *(page 103)*.

Making and Installing the Lining

1 Marking the lining head. Cut a length of lining timber 160 mm longer than the door width. At a point half the door width from the centre of the lining, use a combination square to mark a straight line across the face and sides of the lining *(right)*. Mark a parallel line 10 mm—one third of the lining thickness—towards the end *(inset)*. Using a mortise gauge set to the same measurement, score the sides of the lining to join the parallel lines. Mark the opposite end of the lining head in the same way.

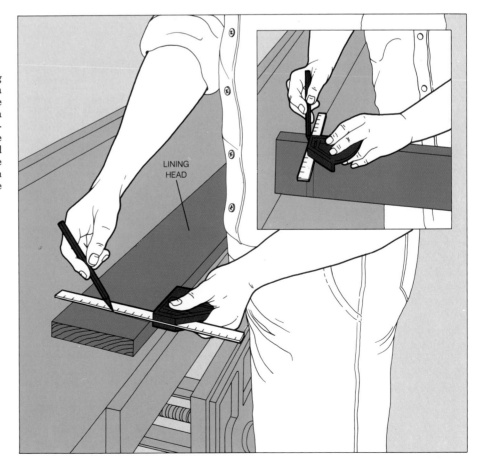

LINING HEAD

2 **Cutting the grooves.** Secure one end of the lining head in a vice with the marked lines upwards. With a tenon saw, saw down the parallel lines on the sides to the scored lines. Using a mallet and wood chisel with its bevel upwards, chop out the waste between the sawn lines half-way across the lining *(right)*. Reverse the lining in the vice and chop out the other half of the waste, then clean out the groove with the chisel blade. Saw and chisel out the groove at the other end of the lining head in the same way.

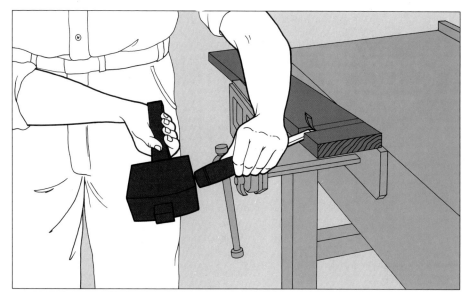

3 **Marking the jambs.** Cut two lengths of lining timber about 100 mm longer than the height of the wall opening—the extra length serves as a waste allowance in case an error is made when cutting the tongues. Mark the tongue to be cut from the top end of one jamb with a marking gauge set to one-third of the jamb thickness, 10 mm; first score along one face of the jamb *(right)*, square the line round on to the sides, then score along the top end *(inset)* and down the sides to meet the horizontal lines. Repeat the process for the other jamb.

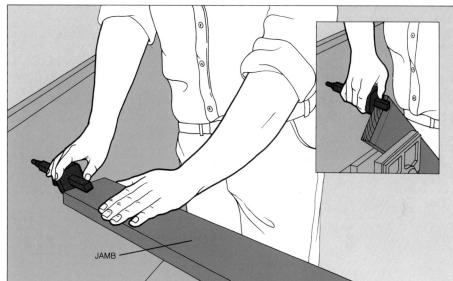

JAMB

4 **Cutting the tongues.** Secure one jamb in a vice, narrow edge upwards, and cut down the scored line from the end with a tenon saw *(right)*. Release the jamb, turn it so that the scored line across its back face is upwards, then tighten the vice and saw down the marked lines as before to remove the waste. Cut the top end of the other jamb in the same way.

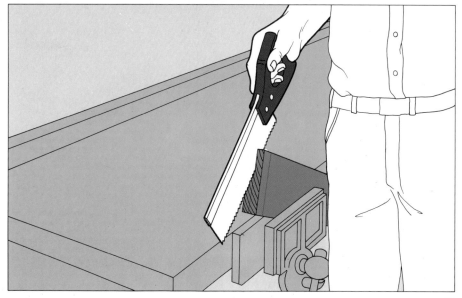

5 Assembling the lining. Slot the tongues on both jambs into the corresponding grooves in the lining head, ensuring that the tongues are on the inside of the lining. If the tongues are too wide to fit, pare them down slightly with a chisel or rebate plane. Secure each joint with two 75 mm round-wire nails driven through the top of the lining head *(right)*.

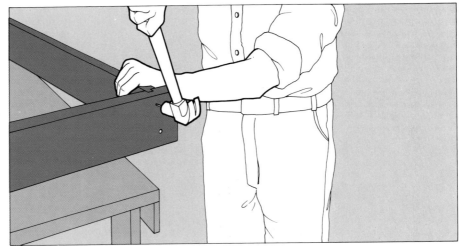

6 Bracing the lining. Measure between the outside edges of the jambs where they join the lining head, and cut a piece of 50 by 25 mm scrap timber to this length. Measure from the top of the lining down to about 600 mm from the bottom of one jamb, mark the same distance on the other jamb, then nail the cross brace to the jambs at the marks. Check that the lining is square by measuring the diagonals between the top inside corners and the inside corners formed by the jambs and the cross brace. Brace each top corner by nailing a scrap piece of timber about 600 mm long to the lining head and the jamb. Use two nails when nailing the end of the braces, to prevent the lining from twisting out of square.

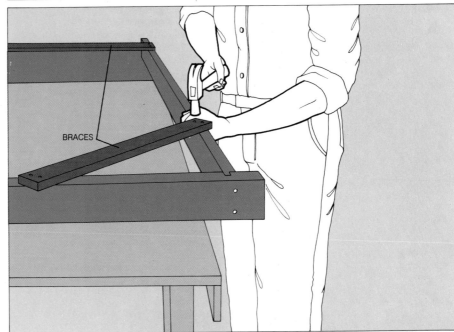

BRACES

7 Completing the lining. Measuring from the inside of the lining head, mark off down each jamb the height of the door plus 6 mm to allow for clearance. (If the floor is covered with thick carpet, allow a few millimetres extra clearance.) Square the marks round the jambs with a combination square, then saw off the waste. If no bricks have been removed from the top of the wall opening to accommodate the horns on the lining head, square off each horn and saw it off *(right)*.

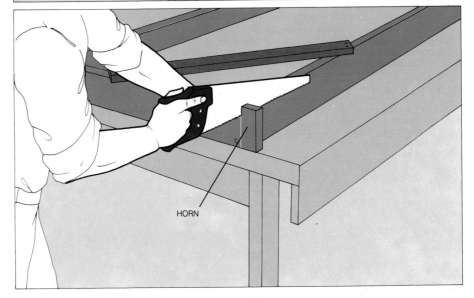

HORN

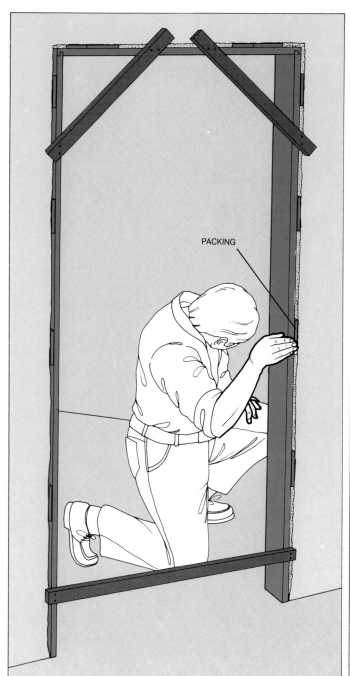

PACKING

8 **Fitting the lining.** Fit the completed lining into the wall opening. Hold a long, straight piece of timber against the inside face of one jamb to check it is not bowed, then hold a spirit level against this to check that the jamb is plumb. Hold the level against the side of the jamb to check it is not leaning to one side. Insert packing strips between the jamb and the wall to pack out irregularities in the wall opening and to correct alignment; the packing material should be positioned to correspond with the heights of the fixing screws *(Step 9)* and the door hinges. Repeat this procedure for the opposite jamb.

9 **Securing the lining.** If the wall is of brick or block construction, use a percussion drill—or an ordinary power drill with a percussion attachment—to drill four pairs of holes at equal intervals through one jamb and into the wall. Countersink the holes, insert plugs, then secure the jamb to the wall with 63 mm No. 8 screws. Secure the opposite jamb in the same way, then cover the countersunk screws with filler. On a timber-frame wall, drill the holes with an ordinary power drill through the jamb only, countersink, then screw the jamb to the timber frame. Finally, remove the braces from the lining.

Hanging the Door and Fitting the Lock

1 **Checking the fit.** Fit the door inside the lining, aligning the hinge-side edge against its jamb. There should be a gap of no more than 2 mm between the sides and top of the door and the lining, and of 4 mm between the bottom of the door and the floor. If the door is slightly too wide or long, secure the door firmly and plane along the bottom and closing edge where necessary.

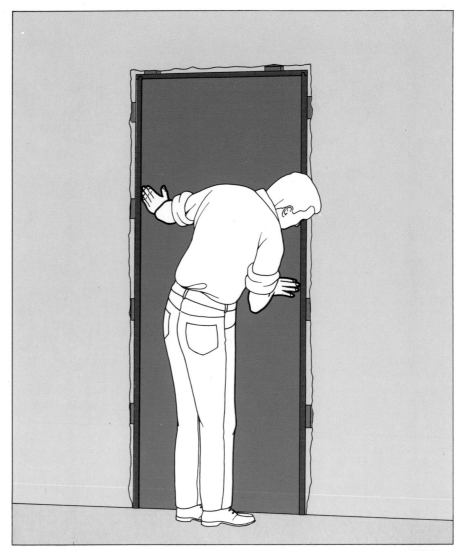

2 **Marking the hinge recesses.** Mark a horizontal line across the hinge edge of the door 150 mm from the top. Position the hinge against this line and mark the lower edge of the hinge on to the door edge *(right)*. With a marking gauge set to the distance between the edge of a hinge leaf and the centre of the knuckle, score the door edge between the two marked lines. Then set the gauge to the thickness of the hinge leaf and mark along the door face. Mark the second hinge recess 225 mm from the bottom of the door in the same way; if required, mark a third hinge recess midway between the top and bottom recesses.

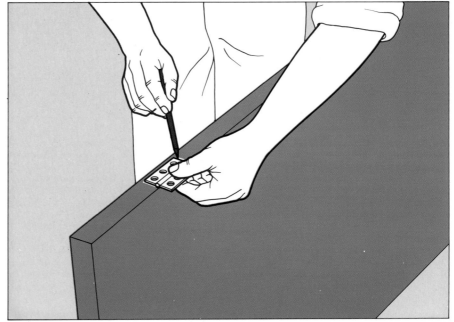

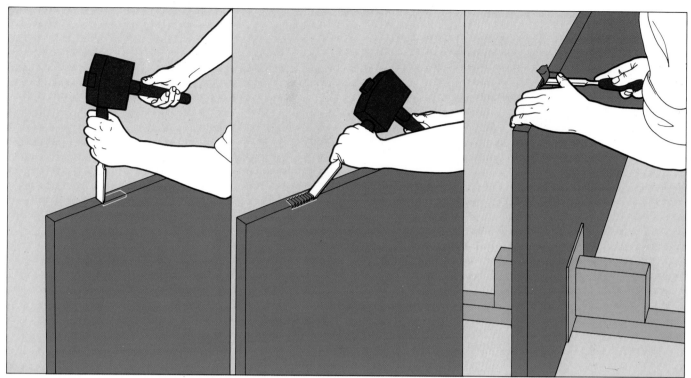

3 **Cutting the recesses.** Choose a bevel-edged chisel at least as wide as the recess. Set the chisel, bevel inwards, across the recess outline about 2 mm from one end and tap it firmly with a mallet to cut to the depth of the mark on the door face *(above, left)*. Repeat at the opposite end of the recess outline, then push the chisel against the scored line along the back of the recess to make a shallow V-cut. Hold the chisel at an angle of 45 degrees—bevel inwards across the recess—just inside one of the end cuts; tap the chisel sharply. Repeating this cut at close intervals, work backwards to the other end *(above, centre)*. Then hold the chisel, bevel upwards, against the scored line along the door face and push it towards the back of the recess; repeat this cut along the recess to remove the waste *(above, right)*. Finally, cut straight down at the marked ends of the recess to make neat edges, and clean out the recess. Cut the recess for the bottom hinge and, if required, the middle hinge, in the same way.

A Door Jack for Easier Work

A simple device called a door jack, which can be assembled from a few scraps of wood and cardboard, offers a handy way to hold a door in place while planing it to size or cutting hinge recesses. It is made from small scraps of timber: three 50 by 25 mm and two 150 by 50 mm pieces of timber.

The two larger pieces, separated by a gap 12 mm wider than the thickness of the door, are nailed on edge to a 50 by 25. Cardboard strips lining this gap protect the door finish during the work; a pair of 50 by 25s, nailed across the bottom of the assembly and tacked to the floor, stabilize the jack and raise it above the floor. When the door is set into the jack, its weight forces the middle of the flexible 50 by 25 down towards the floor, and the larger pieces squeeze together to seize the sides of the door and hold the top steady.

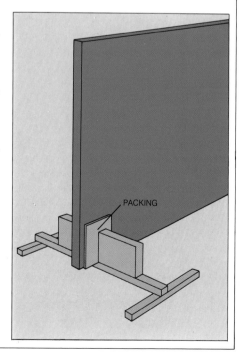

PACKING

4 **Hanging the door.** Place the hinge leaf in the top recess, mark the screwholes with a bradawl and secure the hinge to the door with the correct size screws. Attach the remaining hinges in the same way. Position the door in the lining, with wooden wedges under its bottom edge, and mark the positions of the two hinges on to the jamb *(far left)*. Mark and chisel out the hinge recess on the jamb as for the door, then support the door on wedges and secure the unattached hinge leaves to the jamb with screws *(left)*.

WEDGES

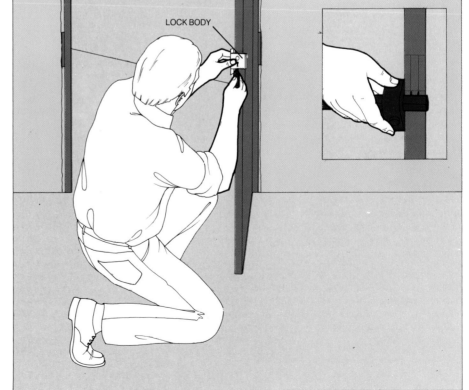

LOCK BODY

5 **Marking for the lock, spindle and keyhole.** Make a horizontal mark across the closing edge of the door about 1 metre from the floor—the exact height can be varied to your own convenience—then hold the upper edge of the lock body against this line and mark along its lower edge *(right)*. Using a mortise gauge set to the thickness of the lock body and centred on the door edge, score parallel vertical lines between the horizontal marks *(inset)*. Score a final vertical line exactly half way between the gauge marks. Set a marking gauge to the distance between the front of the lock body and the centre of the spindle hole, hold the gauge against the door edge at the correct height, and mark both faces of the door. Mark the position of the keyhole in the same way.

6 **Drilling for the spindle and keyhole.** Select a woodworking bit to cut a hole large enough for the spindle to turn freely. Hold the bit against the mark on one face of the door and, with the door firmly secured, drill until the bit point protrudes through the door. Repeat the process from the other side of the door to complete the hole. Drill for the keyhole in the same way.

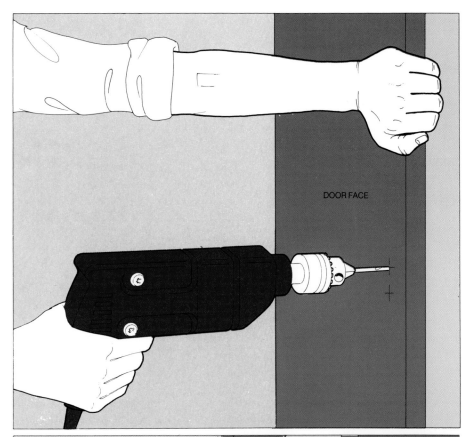

DOOR FACE

7 **Drilling for the lock.** Select a woodworking bit whose diameter equals the thickness of the lock body. Measure off the length of the lock body from the end of the bit and stick tape round the bit at this point as a depth gauge. Drill a row of holes on the centre line of the mortise outline for the lock body (*right*). Use a wood chisel and mallet to square and clean out the mortise.

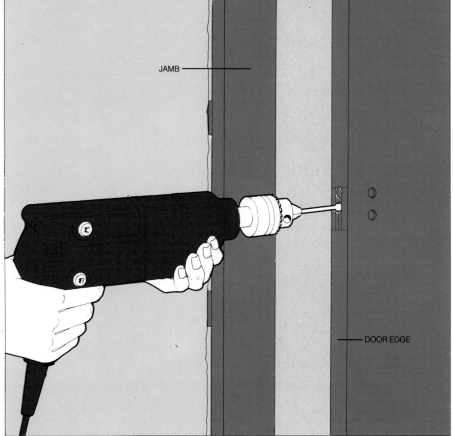

JAMB

DOOR EDGE

8 **Securing the lock body and handles.** Insert the lock body in the mortise and mark the outline of the face plate on to the door edge. Remove the lock body and chisel out the recess for the face plate. Re-insert the lock body, mark the screwholes with a bradawl, and secure the lock body with the screws provided *(right)*. Push the spindle through the square hole in the lock body exposed by the hole drilled through the door face, then slide on the handle plates and handles and secure them with the screws provided.

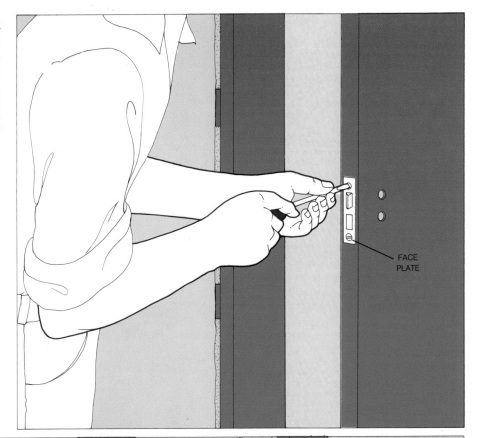

FACE PLATE

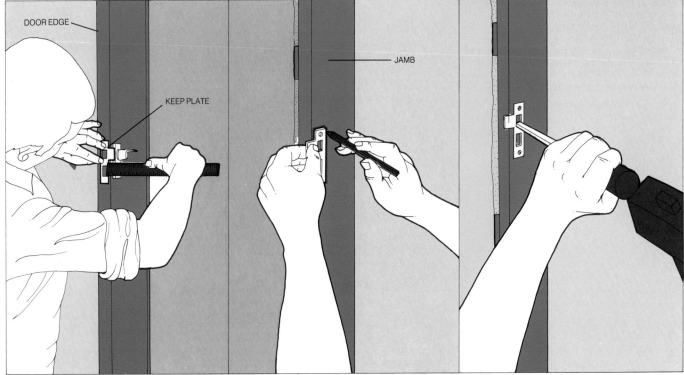

DOOR EDGE

KEEP PLATE

JAMB

9 **Fixing the keep plate.** Close the door and mark the position of the latch on to the jamb. With the door open, slip the keep plate over the latch and measure between the edge of the plate and the front face of the door *(above, left)*. Transfer this measurement to the jamb. Align the keep plate against the marks and pencil round it *(above, centre)*. Chisel out the recess for the plate, then mark screwholes and attach the plate to the jamb. With a wood chisel, make mortises for the latch and bolt *(above, right)*. Tap the keep plate projection backwards with a hammer, to provide a lead-in for the latch.

Measure, cut and attach the door stops and architraves as described on pages 23–27.

Fitting Rising-Butt Hinges

1 **Planing the door top.** On the closing face of the door, draw a line from the mid-point of the top edge A to a point about 5 mm down from the top of the hinge edge B. On the top of the door, draw a second line from point A to point C on the top of the hinge edge on the opposite side. Draw a third line on the hinge edge to connect the first two lines. Secure the door in a door jack or sawhorse slot and plane off the bevelled section enclosed by the three lines.

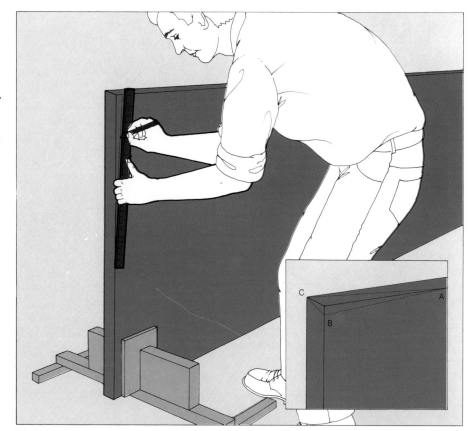

2 **Hanging the door.** Mark, cut recesses and attach the hinge sockets to the door as for the door leaves of ordinary butt hinges *(pages 102–104, Steps 2–4)*. Slot the hinge pins into the sockets and, with the door supported on wedges, mark their positions on to the jamb *(right)*. Cut recesses and attach the hinge pins to the jamb. Finally, hang the door by easing the hinge sockets over the hinge pins.

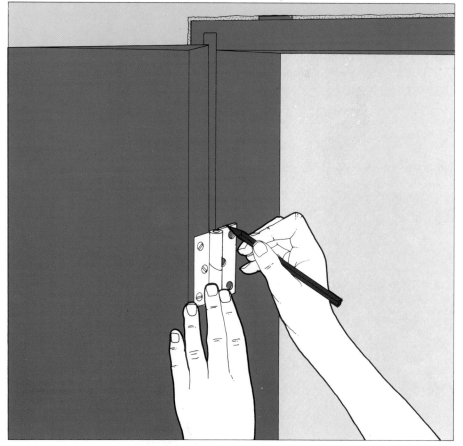

Letting Light Through a Door

To allow more light into a dark room or corridor, a cheaper alternative to buying a glass-panelled door is to install a glass panel in an existing door. Because of their construction and design, panel doors are not suitable, but glazing a flush door is a simple procedure, success depending mainly on accuracy in marking and cutting.

For halls, living rooms and kitchens a long panel of glass starting about 160 mm from the top of the door, and extending to about 400 mm from the bottom, provides excellent illumination; for bathrooms and toilets a panel of frosted glass about 400 mm high is usually adequate. For the door to retain its strength, the sides and top of a panel should not be less than 160 mm from the door edges. Ordinary float glass can be used for small panels; for long panels which may easily be knocked, use toughened or laminated glass.

Timber beading used to secure the glass in the door is available in flush or rebated designs; the overhanging lip on rebated beading will mask irregularities round the edges of the opening. To calculate the correct width of beading, subtract from the door thickness the thickness of the glass plus a small allowance for glazing tape or sponge rubber strips, then divide by two.

1 **Marking out the opening.** Lay the door across two sawhorses. Using a ruler or two pieces of scrap timber nailed at right angles as a guide, mark a line across the door face the desired distance from the top edge. Measure the height of the planned opening down from this line, and mark a parallel line across the door face. To calculate the distance between the sides of the door and the opening, measure the width of the door, subtract the width of the opening required, and divide by two; check that this measurement is more than 160 mm. Then, using a ruler or scrap timber guide, mark lines on the door face for the sides of the opening *(below)*.

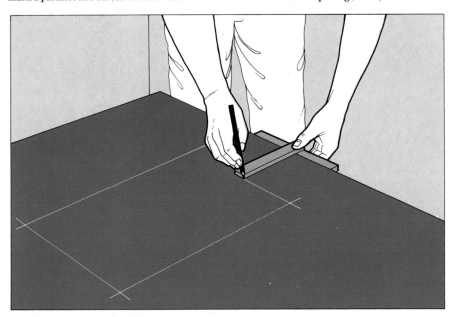

2 **Cutting through the door.** Just inside the corners of the outline, drill through the door with an electric drill and woodworking bit *(below, left)*; push the bit slowly through the wood to avoid splintering. Turn the door over and mark out the opening on the door face, then stick masking tape over the lines to prevent the wood splintering as the opening is cut. Turn the door over again and insert the blade of a jigsaw through one of the drilled holes. Butt a straightedge against the blade guard and clamp it to the door with G-cramps, using wooden blocks to protect the underside of the door. Switch on the jigsaw and move it along the straightedge to cut the first side of the opening *(below)*. Repeat for the other three sides.

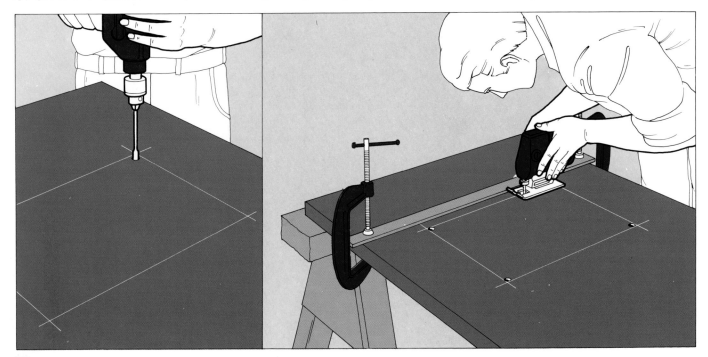

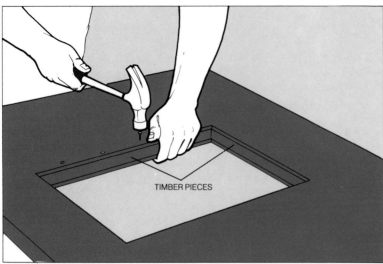

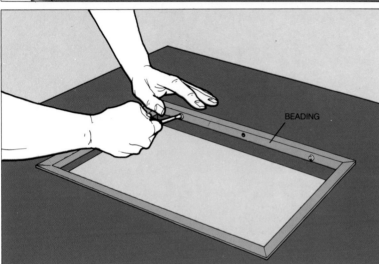

3 **Reinforcing the opening.** Use a trimming knife or an old screwdriver blade to cut out the cellular core between the cut faces of the door, to make a recess about 50 mm deep along each side. Cut four pieces of scrap timber the same thickness as the cellular core, to fit into the recesses. Secure these timber pieces to the door faces with PVA glue or—if the glass is to be held with rebated beading—with panel pins nailed close to the edge of the opening at intervals of about 100 mm.

4 **Attaching the beading.** Using a tenon saw and mitre box, mitre-cut four lengths of rebated beading to fit the sides of the opening. Secure the beading to the inner edges of the opening with PVA glue or screws; if you use screws, drill holes at right angles to the top face of each piece of beading at intervals of about 150 mm, then attach the beading with 30 mm No. 8 screws and cups or countersunk screws.

5 **Securing the glass panel.** Hang the door on its lining by re-attaching the hinges, and peel off the masking tape round the exposed edges of the opening. Cut a piece of glass to fit the opening (page 36); toughened or laminated glass must be cut to size by the supplier. Attach sponge rubber strips to the inside of the fitted beading, or attach glazing tape to the edges of the glass, then position the glass in the opening. Mitre-cut four pieces of matching beading to secure the glass in the opening, attach sponge rubber strips if these are being used, then secure the beading to the exposed edges of the opening by the same method used for the first side.

The Space Savers: Sliding Doors for Tight Places

Patio doors, running on rollers along a track, combine the transparency of a huge window with the convenience of a door; as an opening between house and garden, they unite two spaces visually and physically. A variation is the sliding panel door *(pages 113–115)*, which opens by gliding along an interior wall. Both are practical solutions to the problem of a space that has no room for a hinged door to swing.

Patio doors are sold in kits containing finished door panels made from toughened or laminated glass, a frame and all the hardware needed. Doorframes of wood, aluminium or plastic come in widths ranging from 1800 to 6000 mm and in heights from 2100 to 2400 mm. Wooden-framed doors are more expensive than the metal models, but are more efficient insulators.

The widely used type of wooden-framed patio door shown on these pages has two door panels, one stationary and the other movable, but three and four-panel units are also available.

Patio door kits vary according to the manufacturer. Some kits contain a timber subframe to line the opening before the frame and door panels are installed. Whichever kit you buy, check its contents and follow the instructions carefully.

Start the installation with an opening *(Chapter 2)*; take special pains to make it plumb and square, and allow for a 3 to 5 mm clearance all round the patio doorframe. Make the bottom of the opening level with the inside floor or a little higher. If the bottom of the opening coincides with the existing horizontal damp-proof course

you need only seal it with a layer of mortar. If it is higher, you must lay a new DPC along the bottom of the opening. First, you will need to cover the bottom of the opening with a 10 mm layer of mortar, then lay a continuous strip of damp-proof membrane over the mortar, making sure that the membrane protrudes slightly over the outside brickwork. Finish the DPC with another 10 mm layer of mortar.

After the door panels have been installed *(here and overleaf)*, adjusted and fitted with lock and handle, apply a bead of non-setting mastic sealant between the frame and the brickwork on the outside of the house, to form a waterproof join. Complete the job by plastering up to the frame inside, and by fixing quadrant moulding over the join to hide it.

1 Shimming the frame. Following the manufacturer's instructions, assemble the frame on the ground. With a helper, lift the frame into the opening. Check that the frame is plumb and square on both faces, using a spirit level; if necessary, hammer wooden shims between the sides of the frame and the wall at the intended fixing points while your helper steadies the frame and checks that it is plumb *(right)*.

2 **Fixing the frame.** With an electric drill, make holes in the sides of the frame, through the shims and into the brickwork, at the stipulated intervals. Push plugs through the frame into the holes in the brickwork and screw the frame to the wall. Countersink the screws and cover them with wood filler to match the frame.

3 **Installing the stationary panel.** Check that the stationary panel is the correct way up. Push its upper edge into the channel at the top of the frame, lower its bottom edge into the channel at the base of the frame and slide it firmly against the jamb. Push the threshold step into the slot in the threshold between the stationary panel and the opposite jamb, to hold the stationary panel in place at the bottom. Ensure the threshold step fits tightly; screw it to the threshold *(right)*.

THRESHOLD STEP

4 **Fastening the parting bead.** To secure the top of the stationary panel, fit the head closer between the stationary panel and the side jamb at the top of the frame. Screw the parting bead, which separates the stationary and movable panels, into the top of the frame *(right)*.

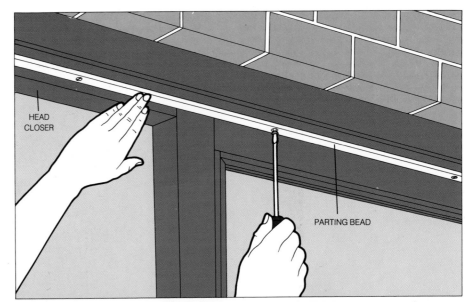

HEAD
CLOSER

PARTING BEAD

5 **Fitting the movable panel.** Working from outside the house, push the top of the movable panel up into the track guide in the top of the frame *(below)*, then lower it into the bottom track. Screw the doorstop for the movable panel in the track guide at the top of the frame.

6 **Adjusting the movable panel.** Check that the rollers slide properly by opening and shutting the door. If it sticks, or is too loose, adjust the clearance of the movable panel by turning the screws in each wheel housing at the bottom of the panel *(above)* until the door slides smoothly. The movable panel should be clear of the threshold on the inside of the door.

A Door That Slides to the Side

A traditional top-hung sliding door can be put to good use in a modern house wherever rooms are compact and wall space is precious. A passageway between a kitchen and a dining room, for example, often has little room on either side for a conventional hinged door to swing open into.

An existing flush door can be simply converted into a door that slides to one side of the opening, using one of the many types of sliding door gear available. For a wide opening, manufacturers offer gear suitable for two-leaf bi-parting doors. New internal flush doors can also be purchased from a timber merchant.

Sliding door gear comes in sets comprising all the necessary hardware—track, wheels, pendant bolts, carriers, shoe guide, stops and screws—although brackets for fixing the track may have to be bought separately. In addition you will need a wooden batten to support the track. The sets vary slightly in design according to the manufacturer: always follow their instructions carefully.

Before you buy the sliding door gear, measure the thickness and width of the door. The length of the track has to be twice the width of the door. Check also that the gear is suited to the weight of the door you will be using. If you are using the existing door, line the rebates with pieces of wooden battens to narrow the opening slightly; this provides a better finish and reduces any draughts. If necessary, remove the architrave and skirting board on the side of the wall the door will slide against, then make good the wall.

Complete the installation by fitting the door furniture—a wide range of handles and latch sets is available. Finally, the assembled gear can be concealed by fitting a pelmet. You can purchase a ready-made pelmet or, alternatively, you can make one yourself. You will need four lengths of timber: a top piece wide enough to give a 10 mm clearance beyond the door, a front piece deep enough to hide the track, and two short side pieces. Glue and pin the top to the side pieces, then the assembled unit to the top of the batten. Attach the front piece to the unit in the same way.

Anatomy of a sliding door. In this sliding door, carriers are attached to the top of the door, and a groove is cut along its bottom edge; a small shoe guide fastened to the floor helps keep the door on course as the groove rides over it. The carriers slot into pendant bolts, attached to nylon wheel assemblies housed in the overhead track. The track itself is fixed with brackets to a supporting batten. Stops set at either end of the track prevent the wheel assemblies, and thus the door itself, from sliding out. A handle has been recessed into the door.

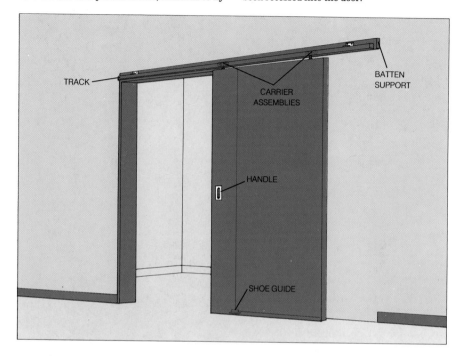

Installing a Sliding Door

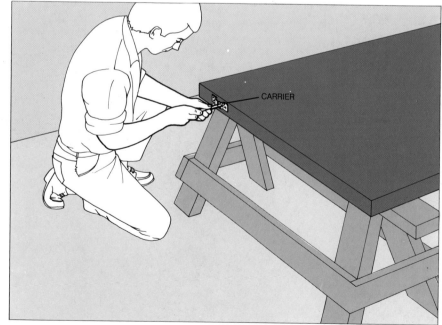

1 Preparing the door. Take down the existing door, and remove the hinges and handles. Cut a groove in the bottom edge of the door *(page 42)* to the dimensions specified by the manufacturer. Rest the door on two sawhorses and mark the position for each carrier on the upper edge of the door. Use a bradawl to make starting holes in the wood then, with the carrier slots facing towards the doorway, screw the carriers to the top of the door *(above)*.

2 **Securing the batten.** Cut a batten to the dimensions specified by the manufacturer and about 50 mm longer than the track. Place the batten on the sawhorses and drill pilot holes. Position the batten above the doorway; on one side it must extend to accept the full width of the door when it is open. With a helper holding the batten in place, and a spirit level resting on it, drill holes through the batten to mark the wall. Remove the batten and drill and plug the holes in the wall. Reposition the batten and secure it to the wall with screws of a suitable length.

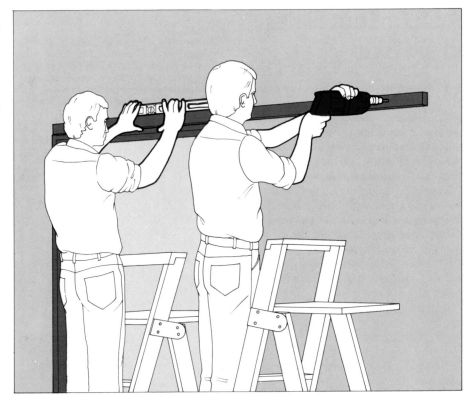

3 **Mounting the overhead track.** Using countersunk screws and self-locking nuts, attach the brackets to the track. Position the track against the batten; the centre of the track should align with the edge of the doorway towards which the door will slide when opening. With a helper supporting the track, make starter holes through the brackets into the batten. Drive screws through the vertical leg of each bracket into the batten *(right)*. When the track is fixed in position, slide the wheel assemblies into the track, one at a time *(inset)*.

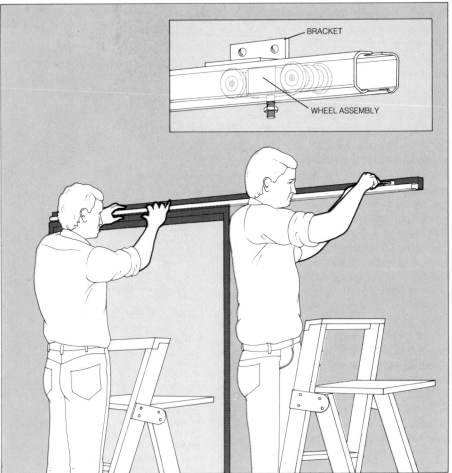

BRACKET

WHEEL ASSEMBLY

4 **Hanging the door.** With a helper holding the door upright beneath the track, slide the wheel assemblies along so that the pendant bolt of each assembly is in line with a carrier *(inset)*. Lift the door slightly and slide the bolt heads into the slots in the carriers one by one, and loosely tighten the lock nuts down on to the carriers. Place a wedge under the door to hold it steady; check that the clearance from the ground meets the manufacturer's requirements. If necessary, adjust the position of the door so that it will be able to travel clear of the jambs; tighten the lock nuts with a spanner. Remove the wedges.

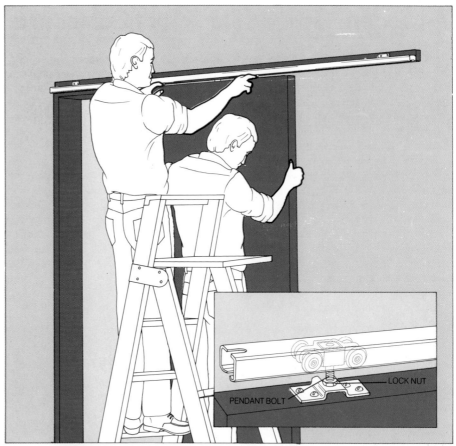

LOCK NUT

PENDANT BOLT

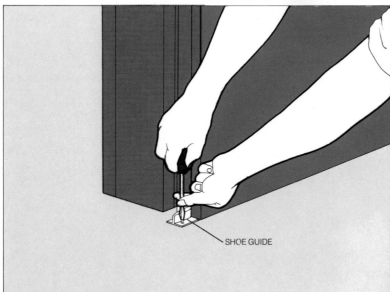

SHOE GUIDE

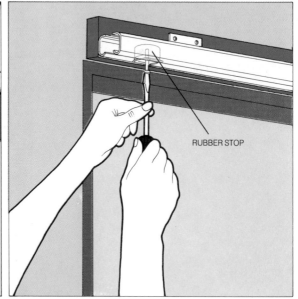

RUBBER STOP

5 **Attaching the shoe guide.** Gently slide the door to its open position, making sure that it does not slide off the track. Place the shoe guide on the floor to the side of the opening, just in front of the wall. Check that it is directly in line with the groove cut into the bottom edge of the door. Using a bradawl, start holes in the floor at the fixing points, then screw the guide to the floor. For a concrete floor, drill and plug screwholes.

6 **Positioning the stops.** Assemble the rubber stops and support plates with the screws provided. Slide a stop into each end of the track and position it where you want the wheel assembly to stop. Then tighten the screws to hold each stop firmly in place.

A Modern Garage Door That Comes in a Kit

Despite its large size and elaborate hardware, a new garage door is surprisingly easy to install—in fact the job consists mainly of assembling pre-fitted pieces from a kit. It should take a competent handyman no more than a day, once the initial opening has been prepared.

Sectional overhead doors like the one shown on these pages offer several advantages over the old-fashioned hinged doors and the one-piece up-and-over door shown on pages 121–123, both of which usually swing out as they open. A sectional door requires no clearance outside the garage; it opens and closes easily, even when deep snow covers the drive. The powerful springs that balance the door are high overhead, clear of clothing and fingers, and

the spring tension matches the opening and closing cycle, so that the door works smoothly, with little effort. In addition, a sectional door is an excellent type of door for use with an electrically-powered door-opening mechanism.

Sectional doors are manufactured in several standard sizes. Although it will cost more than the price of a standard door, you can order one custom-cut for an odd-sized opening; this is usually faster and less expensive than altering the opening to take one of the standard door sizes. Your garage must have enough space to accommodate the overhead tracks and springs, which generally extend back from the opening approximately 375 to 450 mm more than the height of the door.

Sectional doors are fitted either with torsion springs—coils that rotate a shaft running across the top of the opening—or with extension springs that stretch along the overhead tracks.

Either type of spring can cause the metal parts to flail violently if the spring is accidentally released, and extreme caution is required during the installation process. Torsion springs are tightened and adjusted with steel winding bars that fit into holes in the spring assembly. Be sure that the bars fit the holes exactly, and keep your head and body clear of the path of the bars as you wind. Extension springs should be installed and adjusted with the door propped open, so that the springs and cables are not under tension.

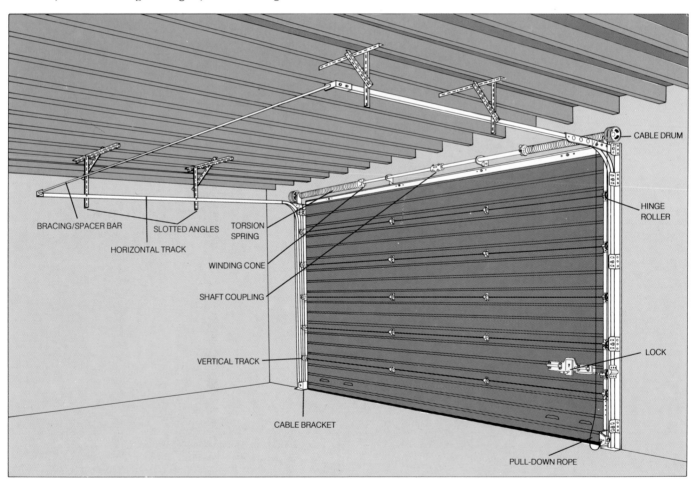

Anatomy of a sectional door. Horizontal sections hinged together make up this typical overhead garage door. The hinges along each side of the door and the brackets at the corners contain rollers. These rollers ride in tracks which are supplied by the manufacturer already set on the frame side members; the tracks extend horizontally into the garage and are secured to the ceiling joists or walls with slotted angles. Plastic and rubber weatherseals along the sides, bottom and top of the door keep out draughts and rain. In this example the door is fitted with torsion springs above the door. Cables run from the bottom cable brackets of the door to drums on a spring shaft mounted over the door opening. The shaft is turned with the help of two torsion springs, which are adjusted by winding cones to counterbalance the door's weight.

Installing the Sections

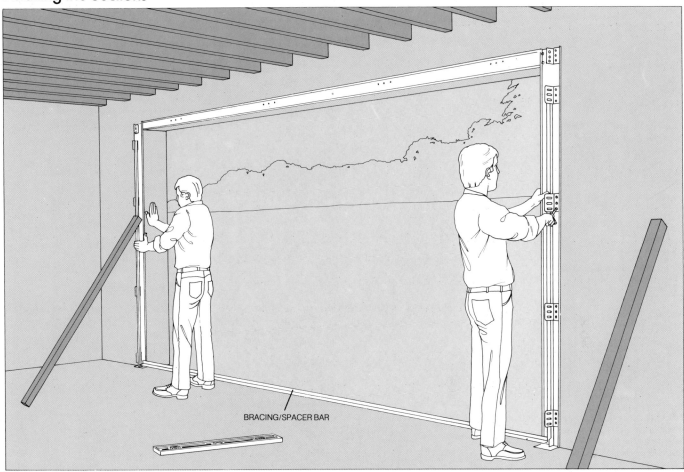

BRACING/SPACER BAR

1 **Fixing the frame.** Lay the frame members out on the floor in the garage, and assemble them with the screws provided. Fix the bracing/spacer bar between the two frame side members to hold them parallel at the bottom. Then, with a helper, offer the assembled frame to the inside of the opening and prop it up with lengths of 50 by 50 mm timber. Whilst the helper steadies the frame, check that it is plumb and square using a spirit level—if it is not, insert shims under the jambs. Attach the frame to the inside of the opening using plugs and screws at each fixing position. Remove the bracing/spacer bar.

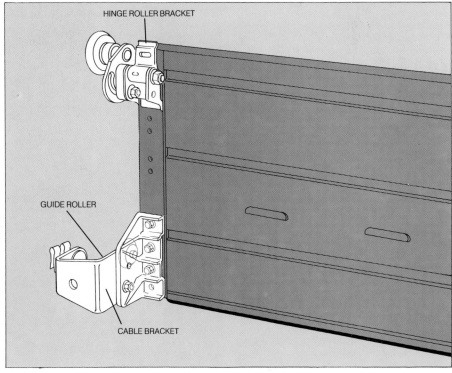

HINGE ROLLER BRACKET

GUIDE ROLLER

CABLE BRACKET

2 **Mounting the hardware.** Using the hardware supplied with the kit (a typical connection assembly is shown on the right), bolt the cable brackets into the pre-drilled holes in the bottom corners of the lowest section. Fit a bottom guide roller to each cable bracket. Then attach a hinge roller bracket to the top corners of each section and finally install the bottom leaves of the intermediate hinges along the top of all but the top section.

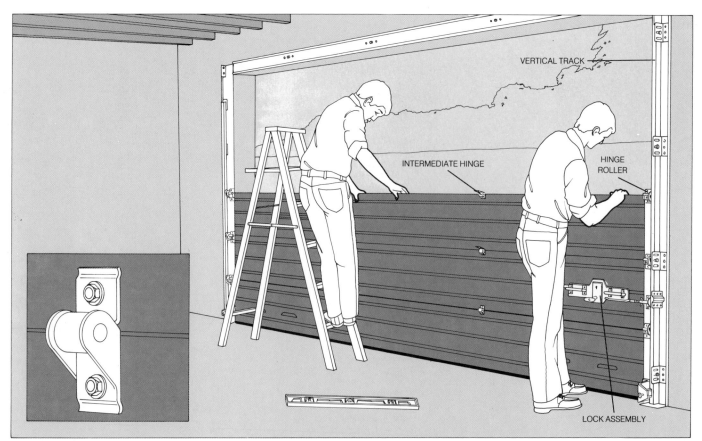

VERTICAL TRACK

INTERMEDIATE HINGE

HINGE ROLLER

LOCK ASSEMBLY

3 **Stacking the sections.** Insert the bottom section into the top of the vertical tracks and gently lower it to the ground. Using a spirit level, check that the section is horizontal, packing it up if necessary. Insert the next section into the vertical tracks and lower it until it rests on the bottom section. Attach the upper flaps of the intermediate hinges to the bottom of the second section with the screws provided *(inset)*. Then fit the lock assembly following the manufacturer's instructions. Stack the remaining sections in the order indicated by the manufacturer and adjust the hinge rollers as specified.

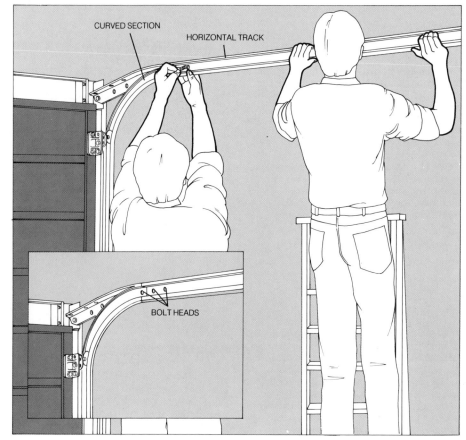

CURVED SECTION

HORIZONTAL TRACK

BOLT HEADS

4 **Putting up the horizontal tracks.** Bolt a curved section of track to the bracket nearest the top of each frame side member. With a helper supporting one of the horizontal tracks in position, bolt it to a curved section using the countersunk bolts provided. Make sure that all the joints are properly aligned, and that no bolt heads protrude inside the tracks *(inset)*. Tie the free end of the horizontal track temporarily to the ceiling joists, and install the other curved section and horizontal track in the same way.

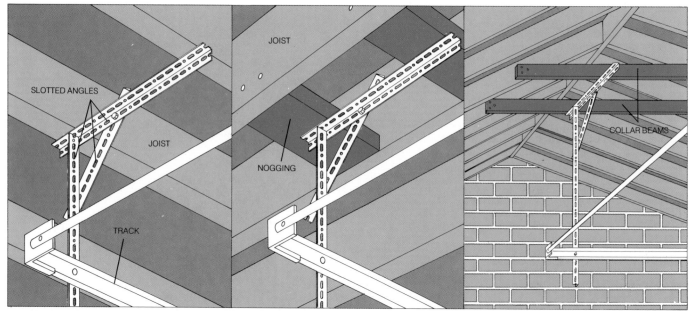

SLOTTED ANGLES

JOIST

TRACK

JOIST

NOGGING

COLLAR BEAMS

5 Anchoring the tracks. Bolt the bracing/spacer bar to the free ends of the horizontal tracks. Anchor the tracks to the ceiling or walls using sections of slotted angle at the intervals recommended, and check that the tracks are horizontal. If the ceiling joists are parallel to the horizontal tracks *(above, left)*, fix slotted angles with coach screws across the joists, just above the mounting location of each track. Raise the free end of each track to a level 25 mm higher than the door end of the track, then cut a piece of slotted angle to fit vertically between the mounting location and the horizontal slotted angle, allowing 50 to 75 mm for adjustment, and screw it in place. Get a helper to raise the door until two sections are within the horizontal tracks and move the tracks sideways to set a 10 mm gap between each track and the edges of the door, then cut and screw a brace be-tween the vertical and horizontal slotted angles. If the ceiling joists are at right angles to the horizontal tracks *(above, centre)*, fix 100 by 50 mm noggings, with two 87 mm No. 10 screws at each end, between the joists that flank the track mounting locations and fasten the horizontal slotted angle to the noggings. If there are no ceiling joists, put up a collar beam to hold the track ends *(above, right)*.

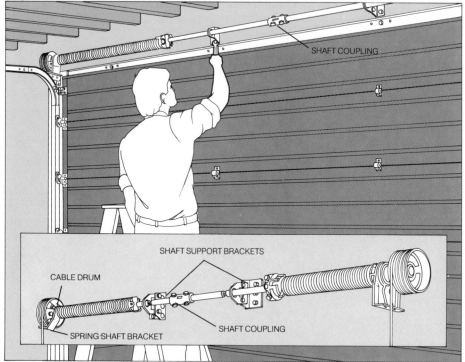

SHAFT COUPLING

SHAFT SUPPORT BRACKETS

CABLE DRUM

SHAFT COUPLING

SPRING SHAFT BRACKET

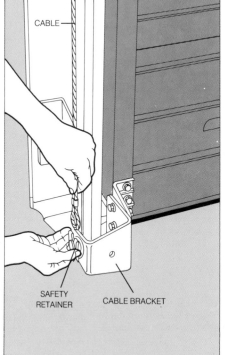

CABLE

SAFETY RETAINER

CABLE BRACKET

6 Mounting the torsion spring assembly. With the door closed, join the two shaft halves of the torsion spring assembly *(inset)* by tightening up the screws of the shaft coupling. With a helper to support the assembly, bolt one of the spring shaft brackets adjacent to a cable drum to each of the horizontal track extensions. Rest the shaft support brackets on top of the frame top member, then fix them to the lintel above with bolts. Check that the shaft is level.

7 Connecting the cable. Slacken the shaft coupling by loosening the screws. Remove the cable clips on the drums, pull the cable down and attach the looped end to the spigot on the cable bracket. Secure the loop in place by snapping on the safety retainer *(above)*.

8 **Winding the springs.** Place a wooden wedge between each cable drum and the wall to lock them in position. Insert the winding bars into adjoining holes on a winding cone and tighten the springs by turning in the direction of the arrows and for the number of turns given in the manufacturer's instructions. Move the winding bars from hole to hole as you turn the cone. To count the turns, draw a horizontal chalk line across the coils of the springs before you begin winding: each complete spiral of the line equals a complete turn. Caution: wind the springs slowly and carefully, keeping your body clear of the path of the bars and maintaining a firm grip on the ends of the bars. Tighten the spring locking bolts hard. Wind the other spring in the same way. Release the cable drums by removing the wedges. Look through the shaft coupling inspection hole to check that the shaft ends butt. Tighten the screws of the shaft coupling to secure it to the shaft.

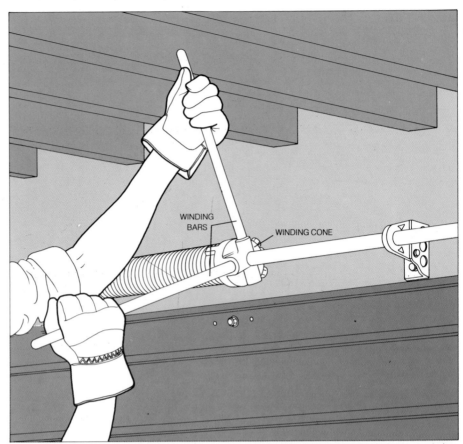

WINDING BARS

WINDING CONE

9 **Adjusting the balance.** Test-open the door and check that the horizontal tracks are parallel with the opened door; the top of the door should also lie parallel to the bracing/spacer bar. If anything is out of alignment, lower the door, loosen the screws holding the relevant slotted angles, and adjust them sideways by 10 mm. Tighten the screws, open the door and check again. Repeat if necessary, adjusting the slotted angles in increments of 10 mm until the horizontal tracks and bracing/spacer bar are parallel to the open door.

Tighten all bolts and screws. Then test the door for balance by checking that it opens and closes smoothly. To adjust the balance, close the door, then tighten or slacken the torsion of the springs minimally until the door operates correctly; both springs must have an equal number of turns. Always exercise extreme caution when adjusting spring tension.

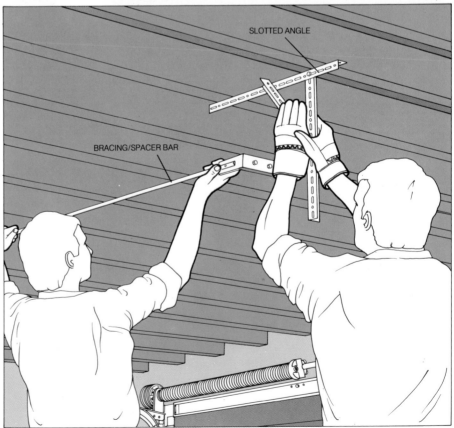

SLOTTED ANGLE

BRACING/SPACER BAR

A One-Piece Up-and-Over Garage Door

A less sophisticated alternative to the sectional door *(pages 116–120)* is the single-section garage door. One-piece doors are relatively easy to install and come in two designs: the canopy, which protrudes by about a third of its length when open, and the fully retractable door shown here. Although the retractable door swings out about 1 metre in front of the garage as it is opened, it then disappears inside the garage, sliding along ceiling-mounted tracks.

Before installing the door, a frame must be set in the opening. Ready-to-install doorframes, available with some door kits, are simply screwed to the brickwork round the opening *(page 117, Step 1)*. For door designs that do not have prefabricated frames, you will have to construct a timber frame; this will also reduce the cost. The garage door manufacturer will often specify the dimensions for the timber and the exact position of the frame.

When you are installing any type of garage door, follow the manufacturer's instructions carefully and in strict order of sequence. Doors fitted with side springs will need a 100 to 125 mm clearance, while those with overhead torsion springs will require anything from 75 to about 450 mm, depending on the design of the door. Take particular care when installing or adjusting the springs, remembering to prop the door in its open position to release the tension in the springs.

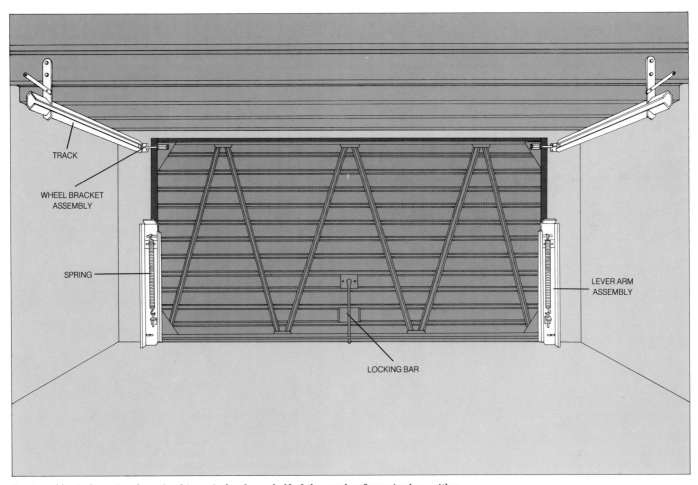

TRACK

WHEEL BRACKET ASSEMBLY

SPRING

LEVER ARM ASSEMBLY

LOCKING BAR

A retractable single-section door. As this typical single-section garage door is opened and closed, wheel spindles attached by a bracket to each top corner ride along horizontal tracks secured to the ceiling joists. The weight of the door is counterbalanced by a lever arm assembly attached to the lower half of the wooden frame jamb on either side of the opening. Cross braces add rigidity to the door, and weatherseals keep out any draughts and rain. The central locking bar fits into a ferrule inset in the garage floor and is operated by a handle.

Installing a
Single-Section Door

1 **Preparing the frame.** Mark the height of the door on the two jambs; then using the marks as a base line, measure and mark the width of the head. Cut a mortise in each jamb, and a corresponding tenon at each end of the head, and assemble the joints with glue and nails. Fit a brace at the bottom of the frame to hold the jambs parallel. With a helper, offer the frame to the opening—either in the opening or, as here, behind the reveal. Check that it is plumb and square and prop it in place with 50 by 50 mm pieces of timber. Drill pilot holes through the frame into the brickwork, marking the positions for the fixing points; remove the frame, then drill and plug the wall. Reposition the frame and screw it in place. Check again that it is plumb and square, packing with wedges if not. Drill starter holes on the inside of the frame for the lever arm bracket and the horizontal track fixing plate, at the points given by the manufacturer *(right)*. Remove the brace.

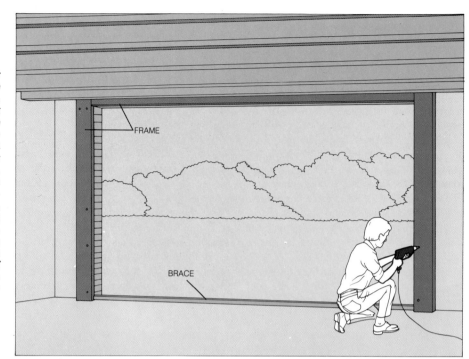

FRAME

BRACE

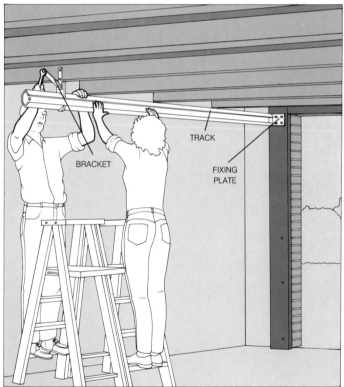

BRACKET

TRACK

FIXING PLATE

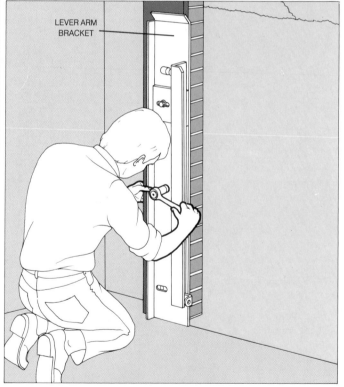

LEVER ARM BRACKET

2 **Fitting the horizontal tracks.** With a helper supporting the free end of one track, screw the fixing plate at the other end to the top of one of the door jambs. Attach the free end of the track to the bracket *(above)*; if no bracket is provided, use slotted angle *(page 119, Step 5)*. Check that the track is square to the door opening, with a fall in level, if specified, from front to rear of the track, then screw the bracket or slotted angle to a ceiling joist. Install the second track.

3 **Fixing the lever arm brackets.** Using coach screws and washers, fit one lever arm bracket to the base of the corresponding jamb—the edge of the bracket should protrude slightly into the opening. Fit the other bracket in the same way. Check that you have fitted the correct bracket to each side of the opening.

4 **Installing the wheel assemblies.** With a helper, position the door in the opening, so that the inside face is flush with the back of the jambs. Use shims to wedge the door in place; there should be about a 5 mm gap at the bottom and sides. Prop the door with 50 by 50 mm timber props. Insert a wheel spindle in the free end of one of the tracks, run it along the track, and push it hard against the fixing plate at the other end. To make the wheel assembly, fix the wheel spindle to the tube on the wheel bracket; align the fixing holes of the wheel assembly with those in the gusset plate at the top corner of the door. Secure the two together using machine screws and washers; tighten with a spanner. Install the second wheel assembly on the opposite side of the door in the same way.

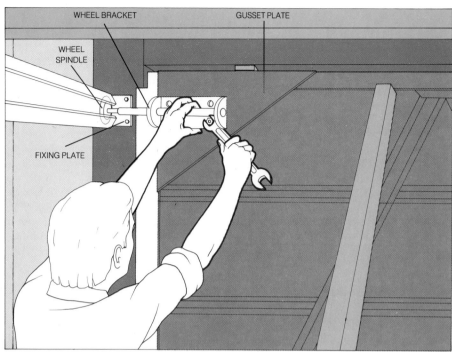

WHEEL BRACKET   GUSSET PLATE

WHEEL SPINDLE

FIXING PLATE

GUSSET PLATE

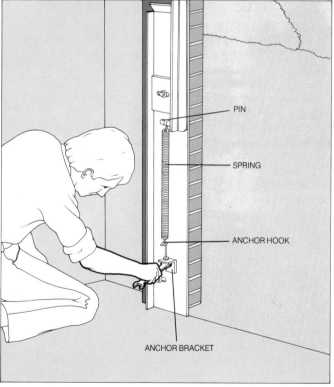

PIN

SPRING

ANCHOR HOOK

ANCHOR BRACKET

5 **Completing the door installation.** Holding one of the lever arms parallel to the door, secure the arm's bottom bracket to the gusset plate attached to the door, using machine screws and washers *(above)*. Repeat the procedure for the other lever arm, then fit a doorstop to the end of each horizontal track. Raise the door into the fully open position and prop it securely.

6 **Securing the springs.** Attach the top end of a spring to the horizontal pin inside one of the lever arms. Secure an anchor hook to the anchor bracket using nuts, then slip the bottom end of the spring over the anchor hook. Attach the other spring in the same way. Remove the props and test close and open the door. If necessary, correct the spring tension by first opening the door then adjusting the anchor hook nuts slightly. Fit the door handle and lock assemblies.

Picture Credits

Acknowledgements

The editors would like to thank the following: Allmand-Smith Limited, Macclesfield, Cheshire; Apex Sliding Door Gear, Birkenhead, Merseyside; Bowater Joinery Limited, Halstead, Essex; Mike Brown, London; Draughtproofing Advisory Association, Haslemere, Surrey; B. Dumenil s.a., Boisguillaume, France; Timothy Fraser, London; Henderson Doorsystems, Romford, Essex; Hillaldam Coburn Limited, Surbiton, Surrey; Hörmann (UK) Limited, Whetstone, Leicester; Derek Hulley, Solihull, West Midlands; Magnet & Southerns Ltd., Keighley, West Yorkshire; John Man, Oxford; Caroline Manyon, London; Marley Buildings Limited, Guildford, Surrey; Barry Pickard, Boston, Lincolnshire; Rawlplug Co. Ltd., London; Vicki Robinson, London; Tomex Windows Ltd., Norwich; Viga Dør-System, Denmark; Yale Security Products Limited, Willenhall, West Midlands.

Index/Glossary

Included in this index are definitions of some of the typical terms used in this book. Page references in italics indicate an illustration of the subject mentioned.

Adjustable steel prop, using, 50, *54*, *55*, 61
Aluminium window frame: finishes to, 76; maintenance, 8, 44, 76; for secondary glazing, *72–74*; susceptibility to condensation, 76. *See also* Casement window
Angle bracket, attaching, *62*
Angle grinder: *power tool with a rigid abrasive disc for cutting masonry and other hard materials;* using to score mortar joints, *61*; using to trim tiles, *83*
Apron: definition, 13
Architrave, 23; adding plinth block to, *25*; definition, 13; lock-nailing joints, *26*; measuring, *24*, *25*; mitring joints, 23, *24*, *25*; moulding for, 23; nailing, 23, *25*, *26*; removing nails from, *23*, *66*; trimming and securing (on pre-hung unit), 94, *96*
Astragal: definition, 13

Base plate, *51*

Bat, brick: *segment of a cut brick;* making, 61
Bead, *see* Parting bead; Staff bead
Beading, timber: *timber strip nailed or screwed to the rebate in a window to secure the glazing;* 108; attaching, *109*; removing, 35
Bearings: *the part of a wall structure that supports the end of a lintel;* making, 62
Beeswax block, using, *11*
Blind, *see* Roller blind; Venetian blind
Block, glass, 39; removing broken, *39*; replacing, *39*
Block plane, 18
Block wall: breaking through, *see* Masonry wall, breaking through; cavity, 50, *51*; solid, *50*
Blowlamp; stripping paint with, 44, *45*
Bolster: *broad-bladed chisel for cutting masonry;* using, 49, *56*, *61*
Bonder: *long stone that extends over half way across a stone wall to strengthen the structure;* *50*
Boot lintel, *57*
Box mould: making for concrete sill, *58–59*
Breather paper: *type of paper that allows water vapour to pass through it in one direction but not in the opposite direction; 51*

Brick: cutting, *61*
Brick-clad timber-stud wall, *see* Stud wall, brick-clad
Brick veneer: cutting through, *61–62*
Brick wall: breaking through, *see* Masonry wall, breaking through; cavity, *51*; solid, *50*
Brush, paint: for doors, *46*; for windows, *46*, *47*
Brush-pile draught-excluder, *40*
Building regulations, 49, 51, 84

Casement window, 8; anatomy of, *9*; causes of sagging sash, 8; coping side stop, *27*; cutting new architrave for, *24–26*; installing pre-hung unit, *78–81*; nailing architrave, 23; nailing stop, 23, *27*; painting, 44, *46*, *47*; pivoted, 76, *77*; removing, *66–67*; removing architrave, 23; removing sash, *66*; removing stop, 23; repairing loose corner, 8, *12*; with roller blind, 76, *77*; staining, 44, *47*; varnishing, 44, *47*; warped sash, 8, *21–22*; weatherstripping, 40, *41*. *See also*

Window; Window sill
Caulking: *flexible sealant used to fill small gaps and cracks*; renewing, 44
Caulking gun, using, *41*
Cavity wall, 50; brick and block, *51*; centring window frame in, 60; damp-proof course in, *51, 54, 57*; installing lintel in, 54, *57*; making doorway in, 54; timber frame with brick veneer, 50, *51*
Cold chisel, using, *56, 61, 66*
Concrete mix: for lintel, *57*; for window sill, *59*
Coping saw, using, *17, 27*
Cord, sash, *see* Sash cord
Crack: filling, 28, *45*
Cripple stud: *short vertical stud above or below an opening in a timber-frame wall*; 52; installing, *53*
Crowbar, using, *66, 67*
Cylinder lock, 97; fitting, *104, 105, 106*

Damp-proof course (DPC): *layer of impermeable material installed just above ground level in external walls to prevent moisture rising*; beneath patio door, 110; in block wall, *50*; in cavity wall, *51, 54, 57*; in timber-stud wall, *51, 63*
Damp-proof membrane: installing, *57*
Door: adding new stops, *27*; attaching aluminium threshold, *43*; attaching weather bar, *43*; causes of sagging, 18; causes of sticking, 18; cutting new architrave, *24–26*; drilling for lock, spindle and keyhole, *105*; filing keep plate, 18, *20*; filling cracks in, 44, *45*; fitting draught excluder, *40, 41, 42*; fitting hinge, 98, *102, 103, 107*; fixing keep plate, *106*; flush, *18*; hanging, *104*; installing glass panel in, *108–109*; installing plinth block, *25*; making and installing lining for, *93, 98–101*; marking for lock, spindle and keyhole, *104*; painting, 44, *46*; panel, *18*; planing, 18, *21*, 98, *107*; planing rebate stop, 18, *21–22*; pre-hung unit, *see* Door set kit; remedies for rattling, *18*; removing architrave, *23*; removing old lining, *66–67*; removing rebate stop, *23*; repositioning rebate stop, *18*; resetting hinge, 18, *20*; sizes, 98; sliding, *see* Patio door kit, Sliding door; staining, 44, *47*; stripping, 44, *45*; varnishing, 44, *47*; warped, 18, *21–22*; weatherstripping, *40–43*. *See also* Doorway; Garage door
Door jack: *support frame to hold door vertical while one edge is being planed or chiselled*; 98; constructing, *103*
Door lining: assembling, *100*; bracing, *100*; cutting groove, *99*; cutting tongue, *99*; fitting in wall opening, *101*; hanging door in, *102–104*; marking head, *98*; marking jamb, *99*; removing, *66–67*; securing, *101*; timber for, 98. *See also* Door set kit
Door set kit, 93; assembling lining, *95*; components, *94*; dimensions, *94*; fitting lining in wall, *95*; hanging door, *96*; positioning lining, *94*; securing architrave, *96*; securing lining, *95*; sizes, 94; trimming architrave, *96*
Doorstop, planted: *strip of timber secured to a door lining against which the door closes*; 18, 23; butt joint for, 23, *27*; removing, *23*; replacing, *27*; scribed joint for, 23, *27*
Doorstop, rebated: *rebate in a door frame or lining against which the door closes*; 18; planing for warped door, 18, *21–22*
Doorway: making opening for in brick-clad timber stud wall, 49, *61–63*; in cavity wall, 54; in load-bearing stud wall, *63–64*; in masonry wall, *54–57*; in stud partition wall, *52–53*
Dormer window, 71; anatomy of, *84*; building regulations regarding, 84; cladding cheek, 84, *90*; corner post, *86–87*; cutting opening in roof, *68–69*; fitting cross ceiling joist, *89*; fixing side ceiling joist, *88*; inserting sill, *88*; installing cheek stud, *89*; installing decking, *90*; installing window, *78–81*; making drip batten, *91*; making fascia board, *91*; making layer board, *91*; putting on head, *87*; putting in trimmers, *85*; reinforcing side rafters, *85*; roofing, *91*; safety precautions when installing, 84; timber for, 84; weatherproofing, *91*
Double glazing, 71, 72; fitting aluminium sliding frames, *72–74*; fitting hinged frame, *74*; installing sealed unit, *75*
DPC, *see* Damp-proof course
Draught excluder, *see* Weatherstripping
Drip groove: *groove under the projecting edge of a window sill that prevents water from running back to the wall*; 9, 58; cleaning out, 28; cutting new, *30*
Drip moulding: *grooved moulding in a window frame designed to deflect rainwater*; 9
Dry partitioning: *building without mortar or plastering, as in timber-frame*

partition walls; 50

Electricity cable: rerouting, 51
English bond: *type of regular pattern used in laying a brick wall*; 50

False tenon, 8; fitting on window, *12*
Fanlight, 9; definition, 13
Feather: *timber strip separating sash weights in a sash window*; 9
Fixed light: *window or section of a window that does not open*; 8, 9; removing glass from, *66*
Flashing; allowance for, 68; definition, 13; fitting, 82, *83*
Flush door, 93; anatomy of, *18*; converting into sliding, 113; painting sequence, *46*; sizes, 94. *See* Door
Foam rubber weatherstripping, 40
Form, building, 57

Garage door, 116; anatomy of sectional, *116*; anatomy of single-section, *121*; installing sectional, 116, *117–120*; installing single-section, *122–123*
Gas pipe: rerouting, 51
G-cramp, using, *30, 108*
Glass: cutting curved pane, 7, *37*; cutting large pane, 34; cutting rectangular pane, *35–36*; determining size of new pane, 34; installing insulating, *75*; installing panel in door, *108–109*; removing broken pane, *34–35*; safety precautions, 34; for secondary glazing, 72; setting in wooden sash, *38*; smoothing rough edges, *36*; storing, 34; transporting, 34
Glass block, 39; removing broken, *39*; replacing, *39*
Glass cutters, carbide-tipped, 34; practising with, 34; using, *35–36*; using for curves, 7, *37*
Glass pliers, 34; using 7, *37*
Glazing bar, 9, *16*; definition, 13; replacing, 16, *17*; splicing, *17*
Glazing clip: *type of glazing sprig for metal windows*; 34
Glazing sprig: *headless nail driven into the rebate of a window to hold the glazing*; 34; inserting, *38*; removing, *35*
Groove: cutting, 42

Hacking knife: *tool used to remove old putty from a window*; using, *35*
Handle, door, 98; drilling for spindle, *105*; marking position of spindle, *104*; securing, *106*
Head plate, *51, 52*

Header, 49, 52; definition, 13; installing, 53

Hinge, door: cutting recess for, *103*; fitting rising-butt, 98, *107*; marking recess for, *102*; number required, 98; shimming, 18, *20*; tightening loose screws in, 18, *20*

Hot-air paint stripper, 44

Insulating glass: installing, *75*
Insulation, *see* Double glazing; Weatherstripping

Jack, door, *see* Door jack
Jack plane, using, 18, *21*
Jack stud: *vertical stud used to frame an opening in a timber-frame wall*; 61; positioning, *63*; putting in, *64*
Jamb, 9; definition, 13; removing, *66*. *See* Door lining
Jigsaw, using, *108*
Joinery terms, 13
Jointing compound, 52; applying, 52, *53*
Jointing tape, using, 52, *53*
Joint: lock-nailing, *26*; mitring, *24*

Keep plate: *metal plate secured to a door jamb with holes to receive door latch and bolt*; filing, 18, *20*; fixing, *106*; repositioning, 18
Kerf: definition, 13
Keyhole: drilling, *105*; marking position of, *104*

Light: definition, 13
Lining, door, *see* Door lining
Lintel, 49, 50; boot-shaped, *57*; casting concrete on site, *57*; cutting channel for, *56* (in masonry wall), *61* (in brick veneer); definition, 13; installing, *57*; L-shaped steel, *57*; marking position of, *54*
Lock: cylinder, 97; cylinder deadlatch, *97*; drilling hole for, *105*; marking position of, *104*; mortise, 97; securing, *106*
Lock block: *timber block secured to stile of a hollow-core door in which a mortise lock can be fixed*; 18
Lock-nailing, *26*
L-shaped lintel, *57*
Lubricant (for sash-window channels), *11*
Lump hammer, using, *49, 56, 61*

Masking tape, using: when painting windows, *47*; when sawing wood, *108*
Masonry wall, breaking through: cutting channel for lintel, *56*; inserting needle, *55*; installing lintel, *57*; knocking out

opening, *56*; marking opening, *54*; marking position of lintel, *54*; positioning supports, *54*
Mastic sealant: applying, *43*
Meeting rails, 9; definition, 13
Mitre: cutting, *24*; definition, 13
Mortar mix: for glass blocks, 39; for rendering reveals, *60*; for repairing concrete sill, *31*; for sub-sill, *78*
Mortise, 16; cutting, *12*; definition, 13
Mortise gauge: *gauge with sharp points for marking out mortises and tenons*; using, *12, 42*
Mortise lock, 97; fitting, *104, 105, 106*
Mould, box: for concrete sill, *58–59*
Moulding, 23; paintbrushes for, *46*; stripping paint from, 44, *45*
Mullion, 9; definition, 13
Muntin, 18; definition, 13

Needle: *horizontal beam passing through a wall to support the weight of the wall while an opening is cut*; 54; hole for, *55*; inserting, *55*
Nogging: *short horizontal timber used to strengthen vertical studs in a timber-frame wall*; 51

Paint brush: for doors, *46*; for windows, *46, 47*
Paint guard, using, *47*
Paint removal: from sash windows, 8, *10*; from sticking doors, 18; using blowlamp, 44, *45*; using chemical strippers, 44, *45*; using hot-air stripper, 44; using stripping knife, 44, *45*
Painting: preparing surfaces, 44, *45*; sequence for doors, *46*; sequence for windows, *46, 47*
Panel door: anatomy of, *18*; painting sequence, *46*. *See* Door
Parting bead, 9; definition, 13; pulling out, *14*
Patio door kit: components, 110; dimensions, 110; fitting movable panel, *112*; fixing frame, *111*; installing stationary panel, *111–112*; installing threshold step, *111*; laying damp-proof course, 110; shimming frame, *110*
Pelmet: making, 113
Plane: block, 18; jack, 18, *21*; rebate, 18, *19, 22*; smoothing, 18, *19, 21*
Planing doors, 18, *21, 107*
Planning permission, 49, 51, 84
Plasterboard, *50, 51*; cutting, *52*; finishing joints, 52, *53*; nailing, 52, *53*
Pliers, glass, 34; using, *7, 37*

Plinth block: *timber block inserted between horizontal skirting and vertical architrave*; 25; installing, 25
Pocket piece: *section of a pulley stile in a sash window that can be removed to gain access to weights or pulleys*; 15; removing, *15*
Prop, temporary, 50, *54, 55*, 61
Pulley, sash-window, 8, *9*
Pulley stile, 9; definition, 13
Putty: bevelling, *38*; lining frame with, *38*; linseed oil, 34; metal casement, 34; painting, *38*; removing old, *35*, 44
PVA glue: *general-purpose woodworking adhesive*; 96

Rafter: *sloping timber extending from the ridge of a roof to its lower edge*; cutting through, 68, *69*; installing false, *82*; reinforcing, *85*; supporting, *69*
Rail, 18; definition, 13
Rattling door; curing, 18
Rebate: definition, 13
Rebate plane: anatomy of, *19*; using, 18, *22*
Releasing agent: for concrete, *59*; for sealants, *41*
Rendering: *layer of mortar applied to exterior walls*; 50; applying to reveals, *60*
Reveal: *internal sides and top of a window opening not covered by the frame*; rendering, *60*
Roller blind: casement window with, 76, *77*; increasing tension in, *32*; reducing tension in, *32*
Roof felt: removing, *68*
Roof window: cutting hole for, *69–69*; installing dormer window, 71, 84, *85–91*; installing opening skylight, *82–83*; pivoted, 76, *77*
Router, using, *42*
Rowlock course: *course of bricks laid on edge*; 65
Rust: removing from steel windows, 44

Sanding, 44, *47*
Sash: definition, 13; removing from sash window, *14*; removing hinged, *66*
Sash brush, using, *46, 47*
Sash cord, 14; definition, 13; repairing when stretched, 14; replacing, 8, *14–15*
Sash lock, 9
Sash window, vertical sliding, 8; anatomy of, *9*; breaking paint seal, 8, *10*; causes of jamming, 8; cleaning channels, 8, *11*; cutting new architrave for, *24–26*;

installing pre-hung unit, *81*; loosening channels, *10*; lubricating channels, *11*; nailing architrave, 23, *25*, *26*; opening from outside, *10*; painting, 44, *46*, *47*; pulley, 8, *9*; removing, *66–67*; removing architrave, *23*; removing sash, *14*; repairing loose corner, 8, *12*; repairing stretched cord, 14; replacing cord, 8, *14–15*; replacing glazing bar, 16, *17*; repositioning staff bead, 8; spiral balance, 8, 76; splicing short glazing bar, *17*; staining, 44, *47*; straightening staff bead, 8, *11*; varnishing, 44, *47*; weatherstripping, 40, *41*; weights, 8, *9*. *See also* Window; Window sill

Saw: coping, 17, *27*; jig, *108*; tenon, *12*

Sawhorse, using, 18, 98

Saw-tooth pattern (of bricks), 61, *62*

SBR, *see* Styrene butadiene rubber latex

Sealant, silicone, 40; applying, *41*

Sealed unit, 71; definition, 13; installing, *75*

Sealing wood, 44

Secondary glazing, 72; definition, 13; fitting aluminium sliding frames, *72–74*; fitting hinged frame, *74*; materials for, 72

Setting block: definition, 13; positioning, *75*

Shave hook: *tool for scraping off paint from mouldings and in corners*; using, *11*, 44, *45*

Sheathing board, *51*

Shim: definition, 13

Shimming: hinge, 18, *20*; patio door frame, *110*

Silicone sealant, 40; applying, *41*

Silicone spray lubricant, *11*

Sill: definition, 13. *See* Window sill

Skylight: cutting hole in roof for, *68–69*; fitting flashing, 82, *83*; installing trimmer, *82*; putting in false rafter, *82*; replacing tiles, *83*; securing frame, *83*

Sliding door: anatomy of, *113*; attaching shoe guide, *115*; gear sets, 113; hanging *115*; length of track, 113; mounting overhead track, *114*; pelmet for, 113; positioning stops, *115*; preparing existing door, *113*. *See also* Garage door; Patio door kit

Slurry: *fluid mixture of water and cement*; applying to cracked sill, *31*

Smoothing plane: anatomy of, *19*; using, 18, *21*

Sole plate, *51*, *52*

Spindle: drilling door for, *105*; marking position of, *104*

Staff bead, *9*; definition, 13; removing, *14*; repositioning, 8; straightening, 8, *11*

Stain, wood, 44; applying, *47*; preparing surfaces, *47*

Steel window: causes of sticking, 8; painting, 44; removing rust from, 44. *See* Window

Stile: definition, 13; door, *18*; window, *9*, *16*

Stooling: *horizontal surface at the back of a sloping sill*; *58*

Stop, *see* Rebate stop

Stripper, paint: chemical, 44, *45*; hot-air, 44

Stripping knife, using, 44, *45*

Stud partition wall: construction of, 50, *51*; cutting opening in, *52*; finishing plasterboard joint, *53*; fixing new plasterboard, *53*; installing cripple stud, *53*; installing header, *53*; load-bearing, 51; locating stud, 52; reinforcing stud, *52*

Stud wall, brick-clad: construction of, 50, *51*; cutting through brick veneer, *61–62*; making framework for door or window, *63–64*; making exterior window sill, *65*; making interior window sill, *65*; removing stud, *63*; setting lintel, *62*

Styrene butadiene rubber latex (SBR), *31*

Tenon: *projection on one frame member that fits into a corresponding mortise in a second member*; *16*; fitting false, 8, *12*; tapering, *17*

Tenon saw, using, *12*

Threshold: definition, 13

Threshold strip: attaching, 40, *43*

Tile, roof: cutting, 82; removing, *68*; replacing, *83*; trimming, *83*

Tilt-and-turn window, 76, 77

Timber-stud partition, *see* Stud partition wall

Timber-stud wall, brick-clad, *see* Stud wall, brick-clad

Tongue and groove joint, 98, *99*, *100*

Transom, *9*; definition, 13

Trimmer: *short timber joist fixed to the ends of cut joists or rafters to frame an opening in a roof or ceiling*; 49; installing, *82*, *85*

uPVC window, 8, 76, 78; cleaning, 76

Vapour barrier: *layer of impermeable material that prevents the passage of water vapour*; 51

Varnish, wood, 44; applying, *47*; preparing surfaces, *47*; removing, *44*

Veneer, brick, 50, *51*, 61; cutting hole through, *61–62*

Venetian blind: anatomy of, *32*; diagnosing troubles, 32; dismantling, *32*; replacing lift cord, *33*

V-strip: *type of weatherstripping for doors or windows*; plastic, *40*

Wall: brick and block cavity, 50, *51*; load-bearing and non-loadbearing, *50–51*; solid block, *50*; solid brick, *50*; solid stone and rubble, *50*; stud partition, 49, 50, *51*; timber-frame with brick veneer, 50, *51*. *See* Doorway, making opening for

Wall tie, *51*

Warping, remedies for: of door, 18, *21–22*; of sash, 8

Water bar: *metal bar fixed in the joint between the bottom of a window frame and a sill to prevent water penetration*; 28; fitting, *79*; groove for, *58*

Weather bar: *type of weatherstripping for external doors*; 40; fitting, *43*

Weatherstripping: applying silicone sealant, 40, *41*; attaching self-adhesive stripping, *41*; brush-pile strip, *40*; concealed, 40, *42*; foam rubber, *40*; nailing to frame, *41*; plastic V-strip, *40*; preparation of surfaces, 40

Weephole: definition, 13; making, *63*

Window: aluminium, 8, 44, 71, 76, 78; cutting glass for, 34, *35–37*; cutting hole in roof for, *68–69*; cutting through brick-clad stud wall for, *61–63*; cutting through masonry wall for, *54–57*; double-glazed, 71, 75; factory-made unit, 71, 78; filling cracks in frame, 44, *45*; installing factory-made unit, *78–81*; installing in door, *108–109*; installing in roof, *82–83*; pivoted, 77; rebating reveals, 60; removing broken pane, *34–35*; removing old frame, *66–67*; removing paint, 44, *45*; removing rust, 44; secondary glazing for, 71, *72–74*; setting glass in, *38*; tilt-and-turn, 76, 77; uPVC, 76, 78. *See also* Casement window; Dormer window; Sash window; Window sill

Window board: definition, 13

Window sill: casting concrete, *58–59*; composite, 28; installing pre-cast concrete, 65, *78–79*; laying bricks for, 65; projecting timber, 28; repairing cracked concrete, 28, *31*; repairing cracked timber, 28; replacing rotten timber, 28, *29–30*

Wood filler, using, *45*

Wood stain, *see* Stain, wood

Metric Conversion Chart

Approximate equivalents—length

Millimetres to inches		Inches to millimetres	
1	1/32	1/32	1
2	1/16	1/16	2
3	1/8	1/8	3
4	5/32	3/16	5
5	3/16	1/4	6
6	1/4	5/16	8
7	9/32	3/8	10
8	5/16	7/16	11
9	11/32	1/2	13
10 (1cm)	3/8	9/16	14
11	7/16	5/8	16
12	15/32	11/16	17
13	1/2	3/4	19
14	9/16	13/16	21
15	19/32	7/8	22
16	5/8	15/16	24
17	11/16	1	25
18	23/32	2	51
19	3/4	3	76
20	25/32	4	102
25	1	5	127
30	1 3/16	6	152
40	1 9/16	7	178
50	1 31/32	8	203
60	2 3/8	9	229
70	2 3/4	10	254
80	3 5/32	11	279
90	3 9/16	12 (1ft)	305
100	3 15/16	13	330
200	7 7/8	14	356
300	11 13/16	15	381
400	15 3/4	16	406
500	19 11/16	17	432
600	23 3/8	18	457
700	27 9/16	19	483
800	31 1/2	20	508
900	35 7/16	24 (2ft)	610
1000 (1m)	39 3/8		

Metres to feet/inches		Yards to metres	
		1	0.914
2	6' 7"	2	1.83
3	9' 10"	3	2.74
4	13' 1"	4	3.66
5	16' 5"	5	4.57
6	19' 8"	6	5.49
7	23' 0"	7	6.40
8	26' 3"	8	7.32
9	29' 6"	9	8.23
10	32' 10"	10	9.14
20	65' 7"	20	18.29
50	164' 0"	50	45.72
100	328' 1"	100	91.44

Conversion factors

Length

1 millimetre (mm)	= 0.0394 in
1 centimetre (cm)/10 mm	= 0.3937 in
1 metre/100 cm	= 39.37 in/3.281 ft/1.094 yd
1 kilometre (km)/1000 metres	= 1093.6 yd/0.6214 mile
1 inch (in)	= 25.4 mm/2.54 cm
1 foot (ft)/12 in	= 304.8 mm/30.48 cm/0.3048 metre
1 yard (yd)/3 ft	= 914.4 mm/91.44 cm/0.9144 metre
1 mile/1760 yd	= 1609.344 metres/1.609 km

Area

1 square centimetre (sq cm)/ 100 square millimetres (sq mm)	= 0.155 sq in
1 square metre (sq metre)/10,000 sq cm	= 10.764 sq ft/1.196 sq yd
1 are/100 sq metres	= 119.60 sq yd/0.0247 acre
1 hectare (ha)/100 ares	= 2.471 acres/0.00386 sq mile
1 square inch (sq in)	= 645.16 sq mm/6.4516 sq cm
1 square foot (sq ft)/144 sq in	= 929.03 sq cm
1 square yard (sq yd)/9 sq ft	= 8361.3 sq cm/0.8361 sq metre
1 acre/4840 sq yd	= 4046.9 sq metres/0.4047 ha
1 square mile/640 acres	= 259 ha/2.59 sq km

Volume

1 cubic centimetre (cu cm)/ 1000 cubic millimetres (cu mm)	= 0.0610 cu in
1 cubic decimetre (cu dm)/1000 cu cm	= 61.024 cu in/0.0353 cu ft
1 cubic metre/1000 cu dm	= 35.3147 cu ft/1.308 cu yd
1 cu cm	= 1 millilitre (ml)
1 cu dm	= 1 litre see **Capacity**
1 cubic inch (cu in)	= 16.3871 cu cm
1 cubic foot (cu ft)/1728 cu in	= 28,316.8 cu cm/0·0283 cu metre
1 cubic yard (cu yd)/27 cu ft	= 0.7646 cu metre

Capacity

1 litre	= 1.7598 pt/0.8799 qt/0.22 gal
1 pint (pt)	= 0.568 litre
1 quart (qt)	= 1.137 litres
1 gallon (gal)	= 4.546 litres

Weight

1 gram (g)	= 0.035 oz
1 kilogram (kg)/1000 g	= 2.20 lb/35.2 oz
1 tonne/1000 kg	= 2204.6 lb/0.9842 ton
1 ounce (oz)	= 28.35 g
1 pound (lb)	= 0.4536 kg
1 ton	= 1016 kg

Pressure

1 gram per square metre (g/metre^2)	= 0.0295 oz/sq yd
1 gram per square centimetre (g/cm^2)	= 0.228 oz/sq in
1 kilogram per square centimetre (kg/cm^2)	= 14.223 lb/sq in
1 kilogram per square metre (kg/metre^2)	= 0.205 lb/sq ft
1 pound per square foot (lb/ft^2)	= 4.882 kg/metre^2
1 pound per square inch (lb/in^2)	= 703.07 kg/metre^2
1 ounce per square yard (oz/yd^2)	= 33.91 g/metre^2
1 ounce per square foot (oz/ft^2)	= 305.15 g/metre^2

Temperature

To convert °F to °C, subtract 32, then divide by 9 and multiply by 5

To convert °C to °F, divide by 5 and multiply by 9, then add 32

Phototypeset by Tradespools Limited, Frome, Somerset
Printed and bound by Artes Gráficas, Toledo, SA, Spain
D. L. TO:1676-1985